Acting Up And Writing Down

Written by Stephen Lockyer

Illustrated by Kirk Bexley

FIRST PUBLISHED IN OCTOBER 2001

by

Educational Printing Services Limited

Albion Mill, Water Street, Great Harwood, Blackburn, BB6 7QR
Telephone: (01254) 882080   Fax: (01254) 882010
e-mail: enquiries@eprint.co.uk   Website: www.eprint.co.uk

ISBN 1 900818 23 X

Contents

Contents

INTRODUCTION

Two Very Different Bananas

THE PROBLEM

Imagine two children, of equal artistic ability, being asked to draw a banana. One has to draw it from memory, and the other has a banana in front of them. Which would draw a more fluid, more accurate banana?

The answer is most probably obvious to those who have ever worked with children, and I feel that the allegory works just as well with creative writing. More and more is expected of children, in their thoughts, learning boundaries and writing skills, and yet there is often an expectation that the child will "just know" how exactly a witch would feel, how a hero might act in a difficult situation, or even how a slave might try to escape a dangerous situation.

The National Literacy Strategy has gone some way to support this idea of exposing thoughts and actions when writing, through effective study of various texts, but as I see it, has not gone far enough. You may be able to understand exactly how to play football from studying the rules, and even match programmes, but will that text actually make the game come alive for you; will it offer the capacity to understand how it feels, lining up for a penalty?

A SOLUTION

My advocacy for using drama as a tool for developing creative writing (or, in laymen's terms, making writing come alive) came about when I was trying to teach how a myth is best written. We had looked at various "classics", had discussed plots, themes and characters, and still the creative work I was reading I considered to be superficial and poor. In a last ditch attempt to breathe some life into the topic, we trooped down to the hall and created a drama together (The Rings of Destiny, Chapter 1).

The writing immediately after this activity was fantastic, and exceptionally powerful and emotional. Not only were the children (mixed ability 8-10 year olds) writing within the context of myth, they were writing with integrity, passion and understanding. All of their character's actions, thoughts and dialogue had a specific function, and every child had taken something from a hastily organised activity and had turned it into an event.

The reward of work like this is contagious, addictive almost. Whether it is an amateur dramatic group, or uniformed organisation, or school class, drama can open doors to new or unusual experiences that the children may well have never been exposed to. It is this exposure that gives children such a heightened sense of reality in their writing.

A BAD PRESS

Back in the real world, I believe drama still has an image of danger and uncontrollability to it. Similarly, in these times of performance targets and valued assessment, it may be seen as a frivolous waste of both time and energy. After all, if children aren't listening to you or writing something, they can't be learning or developing, can they?

This perception is largely down to trees, and having to pretend to be one. This is clearly not normal behaviour, and would be better associated with movement or dance, since this is more about posture and reflex timing than anything dramatic. I don't know of any way in which you could make a convincing performance of a tree, and actually gain something from it. Nevertheless, there are many opportunities where becoming something else in drama can be highly beneficial.

Architects are taught that when designing a building or facilities for infant children, they should work on their knees rather than standing up, to alter their perspective. Likewise, drama involving a change of person, identity or being can help to examine a new perspective more clearly. In the "Paper Aeroplane" session later in the book, the participants are asked to become circus entertainers at one point. I am not expecting that the children should actually feel the greasepaint or the life of the clown, merely that they should experience performing to an audience, showing a skill and enjoying applause. No-one becomes a tree in this book.

EXPANDING IDEAS

One way for developing the drama sessions outlined, or ones that you create, is by continuing the drama itself, or to record the experiences in some form. An effective way for this to happen is to photograph or film "stills" of the drama as it develops, thereby having a permanent record of what actually occurred. The downside of this is that very little of the feeling will be recorded, and it is this emotive payout that is so sought after.

Writing down what went on in the drama session is infinitely more rewarding, and this is to do with the ownership of the drama. The writing of children I have read has always surprised me by the depth that the children examined themselves and their actions, and also by the differing perspectives that each took from any one session. They all showed ownership of their character - they had created it themselves.

This process is akin to a book made into a film. The film is rarely better than the novel, since you had already built up an image of the characters, locations and even intonations, all from reading the book. If you give a child the barest of bones to build their character on (a soldier, reporter, slave), they will add the layers, as will the drama, and this gives them a unique sense of ownership. In short, it doesn't really matter if the character is poorly drawn, or their actions are unsuitable/unbelievable, they are real and vivid to the child, and that is what is most important at this point. If the child's character does something quite extreme, you could always challenge that character in some way; very often another character will anyway.

POTENTIAL PROBLEMS

One concern might be that the group of children in question has some unsavoury elements, or be difficult to manage in some way. Having a drama session just seems too risky to take on - what if it gets out of control? If the boundaries of the drama are defined, and you have some form of escape route, then the excitement of getting out of the classroom will often be enough. One tactic I have used successfully has been to use the light-switch as a noise deterrent. All the activities in the session were to be done at night, but if the participants got too noisy, they would wake the guards, and would then only have 30 seconds to complete the task. The result - a very quiet and concentrated drama, with the option of finishing any activity at any time. There was never a need to raise my voice, and the signal was clear to everyone, instantly. One alternative to raising your voice is to wait, then speak exceptionally quietly, at those nearest to you. Children, naturally curious and jealous of anyone getting more attention than them, quickly gather together to hear what is being shared.

As I wrote earlier, any of the sessions in this book could be continued, but all work well as stand-alone drama activities. It is strongly advised that you don't make any one session longer than one hour, as after this time, children's energy and enthusiasm can wane quite considerably (if not before), and you really want to end on a dramatic cliff-hanger, and an emotional high. Location is also important. All the sessions in this book outline the ideal working space, but most will manage to be as effective in a classroom, though it is helpful to organise some system of clearing the furniture to the sides as quickly, safely and quietly as possible.

One strategy is to say that you are looking for task-teams (children just love jobs), and will choose them according to the groups that can stack the chairs into five as quickly as possible. They will of course, all have a go at this, and you can assume directions for moving any other furniture. The pace of the task has been introduced, along with the team effort required, and all should be safe. If things start getting sticky, then call attention (remember the light switch?), and ask the children to continue in slow motion. This way, you haven't told them off, and they are already thinking about their actions and movement in a careful and safe way.

ABOUT THE BOOK

The book is divided into three distinct sections. The first section offers ten off-the-peg drama sessions that have been thoroughly tried and tested, themes and ideas. Each of these is ideally suited to being used in isolation, but could easily be adapted to become a running drama for a term of work. A diary approach to writing is best suited to this format. This is also the section when you have five minutes before a lesson, or you're at your wit's end with the perceived lack of creativity in your class, and will try almost anything!

The second section deals with approaches to developing your own drama sessions. Reference is made to the prepared sessions, so some familiarity with them beforehand is beneficial. If you, like me, prefer to have your own hand in controlling the drama, then this section will hopefully guide you to a suitable range of ideas for drama within your class.

The last session is, for want of a better word, a glossary, and features some of the information, extracts and seeds referred to in previous chapters. These pages may also help to inspire some ideas of your own for drama with your children. Also included is a selection of books recommended for further reading or inspiration. Whilst they are not essential reads as such, they are all full of good thoughts and ideas, and have proved invaluable to me.

So now is the time to bite the bullet, and attempt some drama for yourself. What are you waiting for? Enjoy!

SECTION ONE

Prepared Drama Sessions

CHAPTER ONE

The Rings of Destiny

CONCEPT & AIMS

The group is a band of children sent as a living sacrifice to one of the gods. One of the group is a member of royalty, but their identity is hidden. Any children that don't survive a challenge become Guardians, and then can advise the other team-members on strategies.

This drama places the children in a situation of dependence upon each other, an opportunity to each be a hero, and to experience a sense of achievement at reaching a hidden, or unclear goal. It was conceived in order to support writing in the genre of Myths and Legends, and suits Greek tales exceptionally well.

In isolation, the session lasts about 50 minutes, and is ideally suited to a group of about 30 children.

VENUE AND EQUIPMENT

A hall is ideal for this session. Essential props are ordinary PE hoops, the larger the better. Curtain rings could also be used, but to less effect. Other props include the use of at least four PE benches (more if available) and any other blocks that are safe to put on the floor and stand on. Skipping ropes are very useful, but not essential, for one of the tasks.

BACKGROUND

"You are a group of slaves, sent as a sacrifice to the ancient Rings of Destiny. However, one of you is a member of the Royal Family in disguise, and you are to help him or her retrieve the Rings of Destiny from the Dark Palaces without detection. Guardians will be able to advise and support you in your tasks, and should any of you be caught or killed, you will also become a Guardian. It is night-time, so all your efforts to retrieve the Rings must be done as silently as possible. Remember, it is essential you protect the Royal Family member, at all costs, even your own life."

The Royal Family member is never revealed to the children, but helps them to focus on working together as a team, and supporting each other. There are four tasks for the children to do to complete the session, but this is also never revealed to them. The Guardians concept was introduced so those children that fail any of the tasks are lost to the physical drama, but are still involved. Many will find that they are at first disappointed to become a Guardian, then will enjoy the prestige it offers. The night-time concept helps to maintain order and noise levels. Your role is never offered or questioned, but you could assume the role of Higher Guardian or Sage. By making the target the Dark Palaces and the participants being slaves, they subliminally assume they are on the good side.

STAGES

The session is split into four tasks, and can be referred to as this.

1. The Bridge Over The Pit ▨▨▨▨▨▨▨▨▨▨▨▨▨▨▨▨▨▨▨▨▨▨▨▨▨▨▨▨▨▨

"A pit is in front of you, filled with sleeping [monsters]. You have material to build with, but it is only strong enough for half of the group, so building two bridges is advised. If you are too noisy, the monsters might wake, so it is also suggested that you only use signs and signals to communicate."

The pit, of course, doesn't exist, but soon will in the children's minds. Use visible markers (a doorway, netball lines) as a boundary, and set the children to task. The purpose of building two bridges is to give enough children opportunity to make a difference in the drama, although building one bridge is also fine. Any children that fall off the bridge become Guardians.

2. The Poisoned Ivy Prison Gates ▨▨▨▨▨▨▨▨▨▨▨▨▨▨▨▨▨▨▨▨▨▨▨▨▨▨▨▨

"In front of you are the gently sloping prison gates and walls, which are covered in a thick and poisonous Ivy, that will kill you if touched. For the safety of the royal party, you must be joined in groups of at least two. Anyone on their own will be too weak to manage the task. Guards surround the walls, so try to be as quiet as possible, and good luck."

To prepare for this task, distribute the props over a section of the floor, about the same size as the pit in the previous task. This then becomes the poisoned ivy. Skipping ropes are ideal for the joining (by tying loosely around the waist, not the wrists), although using linked hands will suffice, despite protests. You may have Guardians from the previous task, and after the introduction to the task, you might want to ask for advice from one or two of the Guardians. Keep your eye on isolated children, and touching of the Ivy.

3. The two paths (the bottomless pit) ▨▨▨▨▨▨▨▨▨▨▨▨▨▨▨▨▨▨▨▨▨▨▨

"Your next challenge relies on you to trust another person in your group. In front of you are two paths to cross, over a bottomless pit. Each path can only support the weight of one person, but two must cross together. You can use a rope to connect the two of you if you wish. If one falls into the pit, the other must also go."

To prepare for this task, you need four school benches. One needs to be going straight over the "pit", and the other begins in the same direction, but diverges off halfway across. This task is best done with each pair going across, watched by the others. There are many strategies to get across, and the children may surprise you with their ingenuity! Again, this task is an excellent opportunity for a few of the Guardians to support the group, through comments and advice.

4. The Swamp and the Rings of Destiny ▨▨▨▨▨▨▨▨▨▨▨▨▨▨▨▨▨▨▨▨▨

"Before you is a swamp, and scattered around is driftwood, strong enough to support you. The water in the swamp, although clear, has microscopic Nippa fish, which swim into your bloodstream and send you to sleep, so don't let any part of you enter the water. At the end of the swamp are the Rings of Destiny. Due to their value, you cannot carry more than one at a time. Some guards have been alerted, so you can't afford to waste any time – act now, and good luck."

The set-up for the Swamp is very much like the second task, with the poisoned ivy, and try to use as much material as possible. Place the hoops (the Rings of Destiny) at the end, and after the introduction and advice from the Guardians, begin the task. The children will quickly assume some sort of system for retrieving the rings, becoming holders, grabbers and balancers, or find themselves another useful role. Raise the alarm in some way when they are near to the end, and tell them they only have sixty seconds left. They will complete!

FOLLOWING UP

The follow up for this activity should take place as soon as possible after the event. The most effective form of writing is in first person, and can assume a diary, or report, or memories of the event. The order of the tasks is not in itself important, nor the roles, and some children might want to write from the perspective of the Guardians, even though they weren't one themselves.

One good opportunity to stretch and enrich the writing is to say that there was a fifth task, and let them create it. With the example of the first four, the imagination that comes from writing a fifth is always enjoyable to read.

It is important never to reveal who the Royal Family member is, or what the Rings of Destiny do. Let the children do this; their ideas are often far more interesting, and again it gives the children ownership of the most important aspect in the story.

This drama session is highly adaptable to other themes or genres. By adjusting a few of the facts, the children could become some of Robin Hood's Merry Men (and women), or space travellers.

CHAPTER TWO

Elvis Parsley

CONCEPT AND AIMS

The scene of a newsroom is created, and details are given to the different teams randomly. Each team has to produce a newspaper to a deadline.

This activity helps children to be more inquisitive about what they are told, to value and prioritise different information, and to work to a tight deadline as a team. At the same time, it also works as an excellent informal assessment activity, or as a way of seeing how the children develop their ideas in writing over a very short space of time.

To run this session, allow for around 1 – 2 hours. It can be successfully worked with anything upwards of six children.

VENUE & EQUIPMENT

This session is ideally based in a classroom, although it is also suitable for a school with an IT suite.

The newsroom drama session requires quite a bit of preparation beforehand. It would be advisable to study, or at least reiterate, the way stories are presented and written in a range of newspapers. It is also necessary to prepare two key props:

Empty newspaper templates

An A3 sized piece of paper is ideal. Each team (a maximum of six per team is best) can decide on their newspaper's name, and put this on top during the session.

Information slips

These are essential for the session. Each team will put a story together, and they will each receive 10 pieces of information, although not at the same time. According to the style of writing, the newspaper and the teams themselves, some end results bear no relationship to each other.

Two sample storylines are included at the back of this book, although it is advised that you only use one at a time. Collect an A5 envelope for each group, then copy a set of information slips (again, one per group). Cut these up, and put them in each team's LABELLED envelope. This is the most complicated part of the drama.

The first sample storyline involves a character called Elvis Parsley, who explodes from eating too many chips at a local takeaway. There are many opportunities for some very funny newspapers with this, and some graphic images can also appear!

The second storyline concerns the building of a local bypass, and the truth in this story is far more hazy, with different statements from all concerned parties. This is much more challenging, and it is probably worth running the Elvis Parsley session first, then tailoring the second storyline as appropriate.

With these props prepared, you are ready to begin.

BACKGROUND

"All of you are working for different newspapers, and have an hour to create the front page of a story that is breaking as we speak. During the hour, you will be given extra snippets of information, but you as a team must decide whether they are important or relevant or not. Good luck."

Give out two slips from each envelope to each team. These will not mean much on their own, but the children can start getting an idea of what the story could be about. After this, give out a slip every four minutes or so. This may occasionally frustrate the children, since it contradicts what they had thought or written, but also helps them to keep changing their views and opinions on the story.

The children will need around 10 –15 minutes to finish their newspaper, and an aural countdown helps to increase both the pace and the pressure on the children. If you have an efficient group, they might like to provide photographic proof of the story, or some mock adverts. These all support the general "look" of a newspaper.

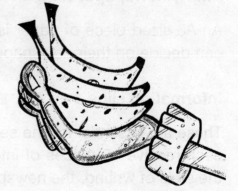

VARIATIONS

If the groups are struggling in any way, it may be an idea to let each of them have an "exclusive" interview with someone connected to the story – this can be done by either someone in their team, or from another team. This tactic is especially useful for younger children, who may not have the skill or the patience for sustained writing.

The writing can be freehand, but this genre is excellent for exploring new media, such as digital filming, desktop publishing or even a web-page! Although all of these may need some prior support or training, this activity might be the ideal launching pad for them, as well as some good writing practice.

FOLLOWING UP

This activity is quite intensive, and it is suggested that you give the participants some breathing space after the session. The reports are wonderful pieces of work to share, and well worth displaying, or creating an anthology of them to have on the reading shelf.

On a slightly more learned note, they are also good for examining bias and exaggerated truth in an English lesson. Since they have been produced by a team, they could also be scrutinised for possible improvements in the writing, although this rather takes the fun out of doing them in the first place.

CHAPTER THREE

Paper Aeroplanes

CONCEPT & AIMS

The children take the journey of a paper aeroplane, flying over towns and cities, the countryside and sea, and end up becoming part of a circus.

This drama session encourages children to view things from a different perspective entirely, and is very beneficial in developing a rich environment in which to write about different and contrasting environments. While the links are strong with a Humanities curriculum, much can be made of descriptive language whilst on their journey.

The session will only last around one hour, and can be run for anything up to 30 children. It is designed with younger children in mind, although with some adaptation, could be used with older children of junior school age.

VENUE AND EQUIPMENT

A hall is very suitable, although a classroom can also be used. Teachers should try to find the largest venue available to them. Some support from other adults could be helpful.

Knowledge of aeroplanes is helpful, though not essential, and it may be useful for each child to have a paper aeroplane with them during the session.

BACKGROUND

The children are required to become aeroplanes in this drama, but plane impressions should be avoided if at all possible. Children quickly tire of this experience, however much fun it may at first appear, so it is worth experiencing being driven by wind before you begin the drama proper.

Start with the children in their own space, and ask them to walk around in rhythm to a clap, which is then slowed down. Highlight those who are walking as slowly and delicately as possible, and encourage a feeling of weightlessness. Very slowly, let the children experience being carried a small way by the wind, and then put down on the floor. Increase this, then introduce a large gust that soars them into the air.

When they are able to create this on their own, the teacher can then begin the drama activities.

STAGES

The session is made of four distinct sections, and can be tackled in any order, according to the mood of the children present. It is suggested that you end on the fourth section, which is the circus, and can prove to be too exciting for some children!

1. Over the town ▨▨▨▨▨▨▨▨▨▨▨▨▨▨▨▨▨▨▨▨▨▨▨▨▨▨▨▨▨▨▨▨▨▨▨▨

"Imagine that you have been sent into the air outside where you live. Soar above your own home - what can you see, experience or feel?"

As the children are moving, get them to describe what they can see below. Encourage them to be as descriptive as possible; the tiles aren't just red, make them dusky or bright red. Let the children try and supersede each other. If one can see a block of flats in the distance, can others see what the people are doing in the flats?

"A big gust has caught us all, and we are sent gently down the high street. What a view!"

Use all the senses to describe the scene below. Get the children to be as specific as possible - what can they smell or hear, can they identify anyone, or what the people are doing below.

Let this gust lead the children into the smoke coming from a factory. Just the suggestion of smoke will help the children to personify their plane into experience of choking or unpleasantness. This is an excellent opportunity to then explore a better environment.

2. The Countryside ▨▨▨▨▨▨▨▨▨▨▨▨▨▨▨▨▨▨▨▨▨▨▨▨▨▨▨▨▨▨▨▨▨▨▨▨

"We have passed the countryside now, and are slowly floating down into a green field. We come to rest."

At this point, allow the children to rest on the floor (preferably on their backs). With their eyes closed, get them to describe the scene around them as vividly as possible. Lead them into discussions of smells and colours, and perhaps even the sounds of animals nearby. Get the children to explain why the animals are making the sounds that they are; are they hungry, is it lambing season, or are they just happy?

Draw the children's attention to the weather. Get them to feel the heat on their bodies and faces, of the wind gently blowing and tugging at them. Make the weather colder, and the wind a little harsher, until eventually it turns them, then catches them up briefly, then sends them soaring into the air once again.

3. The Sea

Lead the children toward the sea, and point out all the sounds as they approach the coastline. This could be helped by some simple musical accompaniment from any spare hands, if available. Develop the sound of shingle crunching below them, and make the children aware of seagulls and other birds cawing near to them.

Get the children to discover their wings, as they become birds, and teach them how to use their wings, holding them out to climb up and drift in the breeze, and packing them tight to shoot down into the sea.

Identify the different sea inhabitants. Seals, dolphins, fishermen and colourful fish can all be built up into real entities, and explain that with all this flying, they are getting quite hungry, and would like a tasty fish to eat.

Ask the children to practise hunting for fish, then the dive to catch one between their beaks. If their actions are too keen, then point out those birds that do catch fish, and explain briefly how well they managed. Those children that are struggling will soon learn to fish better!

After all this hunting, the birds now need to rest. Get the children to fly as a pack into a suitable space, where they can sit and rest.

4. The Circus

They now become members of a touring circus. Discuss with the children all the different jobs that people have at a circus, and allow the children to become their jobs.

Give the group a chance to practise their skills safely, offering support and advice as needed. When you feel they are suitably practised, form a circle of children, and assume the role of a ringmaster. Introduce the acts one at a time (in their different groups), and allow them to perform to the rest of the children, who all become part of the crowd. Let the children respond as enthusiastically as possible.

When all the acts have finished, let the children get comfortable, and review all the different experiences they've had over the past hour, using words and phrases that they have given you. Allow a short pause between each stage, to give the children time to build a picture of that event.

FOLLOWING UP

Although this session has only a very small storyline running through it, this can be just enough for the children to write about. One excellent approach to the writing of this experience is with the use of comic strips, with each picture detailing what happened at each stage. If the children struggle, get them to close their eyes for a moment and recapture the scene in their mind's eye.

The final, circus, activity could easily be changed to something a little less exciting, but it is a very popular option with the children. Alternatives could include a zoo, a playground or an open-air market.

There is an unspoken element of poor writing within younger children in some environments, and this session could help to quash this negative viewpoint. Dictating to another adult, or writing as a group are both good tactics to get something down on paper, and pictures that the children create of the events could also help encourage a vast range of writing. It may be worth writing some of the key words on the board or on the card, for the children to copy down, which would take some of the pressure of writing away.

CHAPTER FOUR

Caved In

CONCEPT & AIMS

The participants are a group of marauding Neanderthals, driven from their home by a fire, and forced to take refuge from wild animals that are hunting them down.

This session gives the children an opportunity to experience a real lack of control over their situation. It also explores supportive behaviour and working in a team. The resulting writing is likely to be more emotive than descriptive, since the drama examines feelings more than surroundings.

This session takes around an hour, but is ideally suited to a longer adaptation for a half-term's drama. It is most effective with a large group of children.

VENUE AND EQUIPMENT

Although reference is made to different tools throughout the session, it is better to have these imagined than to actually supply them - it is just something to think about! A large space should be organised for this session.

BACKGROUND

This session naturally flows on from the almost genetic enthusiasm for dinosaurs to anyone under the age of ten. Whilst most children will have a preconceived idea of what stone age people were like, try instead to focus on practicalities rather than historical accuracies. Although the hunting aspect of the drama may not be 100% accurate, it nevertheless indicates an increased desperation on the character's part.

Desperation is quite an apt description of the feelings the character will no doubt experience. The leading teacher must try throughout the entire session to make any participant's attempt to better their situation become futile. This may seem harsh, and may well provoke some strong reactions from the children, but will greatly enrich their writing afterwards.

STAGES

The different events fall into a clear set of stages, each stage building on the previous one. There is enough potential in each stage to create an entire session from it, should you choose to make this an extended series of sessions.

1. Escape from the Fire ▪▪▪▪▪▪▪▪▪▪▪▪▪▪▪▪▪▪▪▪▪▪▪▪▪▪▪▪▪▪▪▪▪▪

"The hunters have noticed a fire, burning through the forest, and it is heading towards our camp. We have little time left before it reaches us, so collect up as much as you can, and escape as quickly as you can."

This phrase begins the drama; no mention has been made of the Stone Age, or Neanderthals, or even dinosaurs. The children will not know where they are, or what they are - this merely adds to their panic. Hustle them along, reminding them to pick up any "spears, bones, axes" that they can see, then at a signal, rush them to the other end of the hall, to crouch down and watch the flames. Encourage them to imagine how hot it is getting, and experience the heat on their faces.

Without warning, express shock at hearing a baby crying from the camp - someone has left their child in the panic. Ask for volunteers to return to try and save the child. Choose one child, preferably one that will express the intense heat that they are likely to feel from the fire, and watch them return.

With this done, explain that, to escape the fire, they will have to follow the river, to find its source, and they must leave immediately. Have the group walk as a band around the hall, as quietly as possible, so as not to wake any of the sleeping animals. You could add in extra obstacles, such as low branches or huge boulders, but only if you feel it would benefit the journey.

Eventually come to rest, and as the children set up for sleep, describe how they are probably feeling; tired, hungry, frightened and sad that they've lost their homes.

2. Missing Children ▪▪▪▪▪▪▪▪▪▪▪

After some time of sleeping silence, wake the group quickly, telling them that something is wrong - some of the group are missing.

Let the children organise themselves into small groups and go out as search parties, to search. Leave the children to come up with ways to do this, but don't allow any group to find the missing children.

Regroup the children, and have them sit in a circle around a large fire. Give each group an opportunity to describe how they got on, and what they saw. This is an ideal place for the children to describe their surroundings in more detail, but be careful for inconsistencies (for example, plane sightings), and dismiss them as just the mind playing tricks. Explain that after a head-count, animals have snatched five of the children during the night. If they challenge this, say that some of their furs were found by one group, covered in blood, but they didn't want to say this and upset the group.

3. Hunting

Impress on the group the hunger that they are now feeling. Discuss with them the different options available to them in this predicament. Eventually, the group should come around to the fact they need to hunt for food.

Assign different groups to look for different sightings of food. This is another excellent opportunity for the children to explore their imaginations for different areas of their surroundings. Whilst a jungle setting is suitable, the children might bring back descriptions of different locations. This is fine, as long as the descriptions are vivid enough.

When enough sightings have been carried out, ask the children to go out in pairs, one sighting prey and the other capturing it. If the group is a particularly excitable class, use of blowpipes might be more appropriate. Explain that the most successful catches are done using silence as a powerful tool.

If time permits, allow the children to bring back their prey and cook it, describing the taste. This activity is designed to increase the morale of the group somewhat, so this should be an enjoyable activity.

Describe the approaching sunset, and encourage the children to start looking for a place to camp for the night. After suggestions, draw their attention to a nearby cave, with just enough room for them all, and lead them to it. Let them set up for the night, and leave them to sleep for a while.

4. Collapse

Wake the children quickly, and explain that, in the night, a landslide has occurred, effectively blocking the exit to the cave. Explain that the exit has now become impenetrable. Allow the children time to discuss all the options ahead of them, then alert them to a distant rumbling.

FOLLOWING UP

This session ends very abruptly, for a specific purpose. Whilst all the stages in isolation appear to be almost non-events, the gradual build-up of difficulties greatly increases the perceptive thoughts that the children will then offer in their writing. The abruptness of the ending allows much opportunity for the children to continue the story should the teacher choose. They often find ingenious ways to escape this predicament - finding small passageways to crawl through, ramming the fallen stones, calling for help.

One effective way for developing this drama afterwards would be to devote an art lesson to cave depictions of the events. Begin by showing recent examples of cave paintings found in France and Africa (these are readily available from archaeology books or the Internet), and ask the children to describe what they think is occurring in the pictures.

Ask the children to recreate their experience using pictures only. This will be initially quite frustrating, since some experiences are difficult to record graphically.

One idea for developing this artwork further is for the children to assume the role of an archaeologist or art historian, and try to explain the pictures in a modern context. This could be carried out orally, or written as an article for a magazine. This altering of a perspective can have profound events on the group's naivety and actions during the drama session.

If this session is to be expanded over a number of weeks, it is recommended that the children use a diary to record the different events that occur. There are also numerous opportunities within this work to build up a display of literature, from the pictures and diaries, to possible stories and articles that have been produced.

CHAPTER FIVE

Conspiracy
Theory

CONCEPT & AIMS

The children build up a profile of evidence to prove a popular conspiracy theory, which they must then use to convince a sceptical audience.

This drama session encourages the participants to examine facts for holes or inaccuracies. It also helps them to sift through different sources of information, prioritising what is useful, and what is not. It positively encourages the children recreating a large range of information in a short space of time, to do so as accurately as possible.

This session is best spread over two sessions, each session lasting around one hour. Any size of group can carry this out, but smaller groups will have more work to do. *Because of the work expectation and pace of this session, it is only suitable for non-infant children.*

VENUE AND EQUIPMENT

A classroom is perfect for this session, ideally with access to word-processing packages.

Conspiracy Theory is very resource-heavy, so it is well worth making a list of the items needed, and storing them centrally for both sessions. Access to a photocopier between sessions is essential. The children must have access to a folder or clear A4 envelope, to hold their evidence.

BACKGROUND

Some work on different media, such as newspapers and letters, would be extremely beneficial. The teacher may choose to use this session as a good opener to this form of writing, or even as an assessment exercise at the end of a unit of work.

The children are split into small groups of around five or six (assuming a class of 30) beforehand, and access to a list of these groups throughout the sessions will help.

SESSION ONE

Briefly explain what a conspiracy theory is. Broadly speaking, they are rumours built on often-dubious evidence, to disprove an otherwise unquestioned event. If access to some popular conspiracy theories are available (the Kennedy Assassination or the Space Landings), then these will help the class to really examine what these theories are about.

Introduce what conspiracy theory will be about. In this session, it is based on "Our Headteacher is a Robot", but could easily be adapted to something different. Encourage the children to come up with six key facts that prove this statement. Filter out any that could fall apart easily under scrutiny, and welcome the slightly surreal. Each statement should offer the opportunity for further exploration. Some examples include:

- No-one knows what he/she does in their office
- They occasionally seem to run down on their batteries
- An electrical hum or clicking can be heard when near them
- They move quite like a robot

Explain that each group is going to produce two pieces of evidence to support one or more of these statements. The evidence required can be:

- A newspaper article, casting suspicion on headteachers
- Photographs of unusual behaviour
- Some intercepted letters/paper/e-mails
- A magazine article, "Ten ways to identify a robot"
- Written recordings of recent telephone conversations
- An interview with the local residents/electrician

Offer a timescale for each of these tasks (20 - 30 minutes for each is acceptable), and issue one to each group initially. They can use any resource the teacher has made available to them for this task. These can include different types of paper, art materials, word processors and old typewriters if convenient. If available, digital cameras, camcorders and acetates for overhead projectors are also useful. Children are more than able to adapt their work to the resources available to them, so not much will go unused.

Set the groups off on their task, and keep reminding them of the pressing deadlines. If other adults are available, use them productively to support those children who might struggle to support the six key facts, and make sure that each group keeps the key facts in mind when producing their literature.

If possible, clues in the evidence to the true nature of the headteacher should be clear without being too explicit. The children should treat the task as an exploration of expanding and repackaging the truth, being careful not to be too outlandish in their statements. If at all possible, the evidence should be as realistic as possible; printing newspaper on the beige paper used as painting cloth for example.

At the swap-over point, change the task to something else completely different. Try if at all possible to have each group produce one piece of picture evidence, and one written piece. It is suggested that only black, white and grey colours are used for the drawings, since these will need to be photocopied, which dramatically changes the tone of different colours and almost eliminates any pencil marks.

At the end of both activities, get the groups to label their evidence using a letter-code, and collect up all the resources from the children.

BETWEEN SESSIONS

During a suitable opportunity, this evidence needs to be photocopied twice. Some recopying (photocopying a photocopy) can produce a more aged effect on the document, making it seem more realistic, and therefore more genuine.

Place all the copied evidence into different categories, and make up a pack for each of the groups, using a range of the exhibits available. Try whenever possible to vary the packs, as identical packs tend to stifle the presentations in the second session.

SESSION TWO

Give each of the previous groups a new pack of evidence, and explain that they have a short time (30 minutes is ample) to present the evidence in their pack as conclusive proof that the Head is, in fact, a robot.

Allow each group time to sift through all the exhibits, reading through all the information, and supporting any interpretation of the pictures available. It is good to assign a scribe, to take note of useful documents, and particular elements that help to support their case.

Give each group an opportunity to rehearse their presentation, then gather all of the groups together to present their findings conclusively. Let each group present their theories and evidence for about five minutes, and then let the rest of the class vote for whether they are convinced or not. At the end of all of the presentations, vote for the most persuasive group who spoke.

FOLLOWING UP

Despite the amount of writing carried out during the session, the temptation to continue is too great to resist. There are many ways to continue the work after the sessions, from writing a report that summarises all the evidence collected, to writing more detailed supportive evidence.

If possible, encourage the head in question to come forward and answer the allegations put against them. This could take place as a form of press conference. If this is the case, get each child or group to prepare a few key questions for the head to answer. This is a very enjoyable post-session activity, and can help to support the children's skills in note writing.

The children could build the activity into a mini-project, annotating all the collected evidence, or developing some more. New characters, such as a robotics engineer, could be created and interviewed. The children love this mock subordination of their head and often come up with excellent ideas to develop the work further.

There are many other conspiracy theories that can be "created" if the teacher feels that the head/robot concept is too sensitive with a class. Other ideas include:

- **"School dinners are poisoned"**
- **"The midday supervisors are aliens"**
- **"OFSTED inspectors are Russian spies"**

One short activity is to ask the children to create more ideas for conspiracy theories for future use. All the written evidence should be safely stored, and added to in future sessions of this sort as a helpful resource.

CHAPTER SIX

Space Farm

CONCEPT & AIMS

The children are all living on a farm based on the surface of a distant planet. The animals are all what we would consider to be aliens, and all require very different treatment. There is a problem with the oxygen supply, forcing the inhabitants to make difficult decisions.

It is the oxygen crisis that is the main focal point of this drama session, where the children build up a great dependency on each other, only to make a difficult choice at the conclusion. Any activity that challenges the children's perceptions of friendship and loyalty must be dealt with carefully and sensitively.

In isolation, this session lasts around 90 minutes, and usually works best with a large group of about 30 children.

VENUE AND EQUIPMENT

Although a hall is well suited to this session, it might be worth considering other alternative venues, especially outdoors. Some of the session, particularly the debate near the conclusion, could be carried out indoors. There is no specific equipment needed for this activity.

BACKGROUND

"Welcome to the Space Farm, on the planet [Phal], in the [Tinder] solar system. As the only inhabitants of this farm, you are considered to be the experts in caring for the many interesting and exotic creatures that live on the farm. Would one of you like to lead the tour?"

Any introduction to this session that places the children firmly in this new universe will help. The bracketed names can be changed to suit, and perhaps some drawings of unusual animals or planets, prepared beforehand, will help stimulate the children's imagination all the more.

There is real scope for the children to create as much or as little as they wish in this session. In the introduction, a tour of the farm by one of the children is suggested, but the teacher could easily do this, with the children slowly taking over. The main idea is for the children to become as familiar as possible with their new environment. In order for the children to progress quickly, try and identify jobs that are carried out, or need to be done, during the tour. Volunteers can be accepted at this point.

When the tour is complete, encourage the children to decide on their jobs - the more interesting and challenging the better! You might like to get the children to introduce themselves to any newcomers, and demonstrate the most difficult part of their job. This will however be the only performance aspect of this drama.

STAGES

1. Routines on the Farm ■

"With the Intergalactic Inspectors coming in two days, we need to make sure that everything is shipshape and prepared, so could we work very hard today to make sure the animals are at their best."

This is an opportunity for all the children to be very busy with their jobs, and an element of pride in their "work" should be encouraged. Any children who complete their work early could be commended for the work so far, and promoted to another task (decided by them or the teacher).

When the children all appear to have moulded their characters well enough, encourage them all as a group to check the perimeter walls for damage or wear. It is crucial the whole group does this, as they will be responsible then for the next chain of events collectively, rather than be able to blame individuals.

2. Savage Thefts ■

"One of the keepers has discovered that some eggs have been stolen by the savages that live nearby. It turns out that they had made a hole in our perimeter fence, so we are all to blame. We must all help to capture the savages, and save the eggs, before it is too late."

It is best to split this into two parts, the 'capture' and the 'egg retrieval'. If the children are lively, one suggestion is to make the savages quite poisonous to the touch, and that they need ensnaring rather than grabbing.

Once the children have captured enough imaginary savages, then the eggs must be retrieved. Make the eggs too heavy for one person to carry, and exceptionally fragile. A penalty for dropping one could be a forced return to Earth, in order to encourage the children to be delicate about the handling of the eggs.

3. The Trial

Once the head savage has been caught, it is time to put him/her to trial. There are two ways to do this, both requiring a "teacher in role". One option is for the teacher to play the head savage themself, or to play an intermediary. It is advised that if there is only one adult involved, the latter approach is best. If however there is another adult available, they could play the head savage.

Encourage the children to decide on five questions to ask the savage during the trial. It is probably best to split the group into five smaller groups for this. These questions can then be posed to the head savage.

It should emerge from the answers that the savages aren't so savage after all, they are hungry and desperate. Explain to the court that they used to live on the planet with the animals until the human colony was set up, and they were made homeless. Many of their young died, and they have been forced to steal from the Farm. Their belief in not killing live animals caused them to steal the eggs rather than the creatures. This tale should continue until it is felt that the court is sympathetic to the plight of the savages.

Explain that whatever the situation, the crime remains the same, and a suitable punishment must be decided on. In their five smaller groups, allow each group to come up with an appropriate punishment, then let the children vote for what punishment is seen as most fair.

4. Oxygen Crisis

Explain to the children that damage caused by the savages has made the farm unsafe for humans. They have damaged the ventilation systems, leaving only enough oxygen for half the group to survive.

Run a large group meeting, deciding on what to do, and then explain that pairs have been drawn, and each pair has to decide which of them survives. Choose the pairs carefully, making sure that those with strong personalities are pitted against similar children, and more compliant children likewise. Give the children a time limit to decide, hinting that every minute is crucial for all.

After their discussion, make each pair declare their decision, and reasoning behind it. After each pair have spoken, allow the rest of the children to vote for who survives.

Allow the children the opportunity to say goodbye to the animals in their care.

FOLLOWING UP

The writing of this session should begin as soon as possible after the drama itself. Although there are many ways the events could be written up, one ideal form is the obituary genre. This could be done on their own character, or another (perhaps even the head savage). It could be sympathetic, unsympathetic, or even have an obituary for each.

Writing down the range of emotions that the children are likely to have experienced in the drama can be difficult for some, it is worth some time going through each of the major events, and getting the children to talk about how they felt at each point. Their torn loyalties and conflicting emotions are an excellent basis for some very interesting and passionate writing, and it should be expected that some writing is very defensive of their actions, while others condemn themselves quite harshly.

This drama session can be adjusted into an extended series of sessions, and examples of a Space Farm extension can be found in Chapter Fourteen of this book.

CHAPTER SEVEN

Talderton-on-Sea

CONCEPT & AIMS

A small seaside resident's group meets up to decide on the fate of their collapsing pier. They all have a stake in the developments, whether favourable or not, and must come up with a reasonable verdict for the future of their town by the end of the session.

This drama encourages the participants to examine a situation from a different point of view, and defend their arguments well. They will also gain some experience in leading discussions, and speaking in public to fight their cause. This session is particularly effective for tackling issues in writing, such as character dilemmas, or persuasive writing.

This session takes around one hour, and is best suited to a group of older primary children. More than 30 participants may make timing difficult.

VENUE AND EQUIPMENT

This session is quite simple to run in a classroom, although a hall would do just as well. It may be convenient to have some sticky labels and pens for the children to indicate their respective roles in this drama, since these are fairly crucial.

BACKGROUND

The drama relies heavily on the children discussing and examining the different positions available to them as part of a resident's committee. They have been asked to examine whether the dilapidated and crumbling pier should be torn down or not. It would be useful to brainstorm the different jobs that would be required at a typical seaside town, but make sure that more regular jobs are included, since at least two sides are needed for a debate to take place!

In order to create an effective debate, the two sides need to be put into smaller groups, one for the pier closure, and one against. It is worth sorting these positions surreptitiously, to avoid suspicion. Suggestions for jobs and sides are:

For pier closure
- *Builder, decorator, lifeguard, driftwood artist, doctor, vicar*

Against pier closure
- *Bingo-caller, tourist officer, local historian, funfair manager, ice cream vendor*

Although it is not essential, this session is ideal for a teacher-in-role. If this is chosen, ensure that the material is sufficiently familiar, and that any possible deviations or issues that may arise are already considered.

STAGES

The session is broken into three very simple sections; review, discussion and debate.

1. Review of the Current Situation ▣▣▣▣▣▣▣▣▣▣▣▣▣▣▣▣▣▣▣▣▣▣▣▣▣▣

"Welcome everyone, and thank you for taking time out to come and discuss what is going on at the moment in Talderton-on-Sea. As you are all aware, for the past couple of years, things have been very difficult for us all here. Many seaside businesses have gone bust, and we are all struggling to manage financially. For some reason, we just aren't getting the tourists in any more. To help us get a complete picture, I was wondering if one or two of you would be willing to volunteer a few words and describe just how bad things are for you. Is there anyone willing to do this?"

The teacher should expect many volunteers, and they should be eagerly accepted. Try and be supportive to the troubles, and underline any major difficulties any individuals may have ("You have so few customers!"). The teacher should accept enough comments to engender the major difficulty all the locals are feeling at the moment.

To aid any follow-up work that the children will create after this session, the next discussion is advised but not entirely necessary.

"It should be obvious to anyone here that things aren't going to get any better without doing something radical to save our town. Does anyone have any ideas on how we could improve our current situation?"

2. The Discussion ▨▨▨▨▨▨▨▨▨▨▨▨▨▨▨▨▨▨▨▨▨▨▨▨▨▨▨▨▨▨

"I have been asked by Talderton Council to put forward our feelings as residents to the proposed demolition of the pier. Clearly, this demolition would directly affect all our businesses, for good or bad."

At this point, a dividing up of groups must be done carefully. Asking the children to raise their hands 'for' and 'against' may indicate a rough splitting of the group into two halves. If this is the case, then use this vote as a way of creating the two groups. If however there is an uneven sway to one side or other of the argument, then make no particular reference to the vote, but treat it as simply gauging public opinion. Divide the group into the pre-determined categories, and have each group occupy a different space in the hall.

Both groups need to have explained to them that they are to speak as a whole to a larger group of residents, on whether the pier should be demolished or not. Highlight the fact that this may be the only time they are asked for their opinions, and that this could make or break their respective businesses. As a result, they need to make sure that their argument is very strong, with personal testaments if possible.

Speak in turn to each group, telling them whether they are 'for' or 'against' the pier, and only let those who provide a reasonable enough excuse change groups. After this introduction, the teacher should appear as neutral as possible, giving each side equal support.

If there are too many unmanageable or strong personalities in each group, it might be more appropriate to divide a group further, or to appoint a leader for each side. Having a conch, or other object to indicate who is allowed to speak may also be helpful in controlling what might otherwise become a free-for-all.

Give both groups a time limit, and make it slightly unreasonable, since a substantial amount of time can often be wasted in leadership battles and chat - the aim is to immerse the participants in serious discussion and role-play as quickly as possible. Indicate the time left in five-minute intervals, to help the groups remain focussed.

THE DEBATE

"Welcome back everyone. We have many things on the agenda, but it is probably best to begin with the most important in all our minds, the pier demolition. I have asked several members of different groups who either support or oppose the demolition to come and speak this evening, and hope that you will all give everyone a fair hearing. You should remember that we have been asked to vote at the end of the debate, so keep an open mind, and try to consider the effects on the town as well as yourself. Who would like to begin?"

Rather than run the meeting as a formal debate, allow it to flow as a meeting would normally. Allow enough time for each side to have their say in the time allocated. This can be one after the other, or as a volley of views, alternating evenly between 'For' and 'Against'.

Whenever possible, allow personal testament to take place as much as possible. This enables the debate to be centred on the effect of the demolition with local people, rather than any general effect. This will also support the children's future work on the topic.

When the debate has run far enough, call a halt to proceedings, and ask the participants to close their eyes. Encourage the children to think through all that they have heard, and think carefully about their personal opinions on the demolition. Get the group to then vote for or against the demolition, and reveal the result of the vote.

The teacher may find it beneficial for the group to then have a discussion on the possible implications of the decision. Although this is not central to the session, it may help the children follow the story through in their writing.

FOLLOWING UP

There are many avenues for writing experiences after this session. There are opportunities for both factual and fictional writing. One particularly helpful way of channelling a point of view is to ask the children to write either an article or a letter for the local paper, indicating their views.

Another possibility for writing would be for the children to report on the meeting. This could be done quite sympathetically, or could include all the bias exposed during the meeting.

One more ambitious piece of writing could be done from a hindsight perspective, allowing the children to imagine that the events took place some years ago, and how the decision altered the town. In this situation, some support will be required. One way of doing this would be to supply the children with possible headlines or titles to write to. Some suggestions are:

- The Pier closure: A mistake
- Reversal of fortunes - townsfolk have the last laugh
- Talderton Pier: the end of an era
- Hope as pier rebuilt

Whilst the children would not have enough experience of seasonal employment from this session alone, it might well be a useful writing experience after a visit to a town like the fictional Talderton-on-Sea.

The session is of course easily adaptable to any sort of crisis that a town in general might suffer. These situations may range from a new hypermarket opening nearby, to a possible bypass being built. More knowledge about a real location or conflict will support any conviction in the children's work.

CHAPTER EIGHT

Chopper Zoo

CONCEPT & AIMS

The children are a group of managers, in charge of an advertising campaign for a local zoo. They must decide as a group what strategies they must use to bring awareness and/or revenue into the zoo.

This session is designed to help children to focus their ideas and imaginations on portraying something in a good light - Chopper Zoo. They have to work as a group to optimise its potential as a zoo and, as such, design an advertising campaign. The writing task after the drama is driven by the advertising campaign, and often produces some interesting and clear advertisements that might not have otherwise materialised.

The session lasts approximately one hour for 30 children, split into three groups of ten, who will be split in half during the session into groups of five.

VENUE AND EQUIPMENT

This session is suited to a classroom, although using an IT suite, if available, might be more appropriate for some schools.

The possibilities for written work after this session are virtually limitless, so it is worthwhile preparing these beforehand. Its aims tie in well with any IT topics on Presentation or Desktop Publishing, and this could be an alternative for some if suitable equipment is available.

In addition, any information on local or regional zoos would be beneficial. Zoos have more recently become much more aware of the interest children have in them, and many now prepare media packs and educational information, available at a nominal charge. The best approach is by writing to the zoo in question, or investigating them further on the Internet.

Because of the nature of the session, large sheets of paper and pens would be helpful for each group to take notes with.

BACKGROUND

Spend a little time dividing the children into three groups, with roughly ten in each group. Aim to spread any dominant personalities within the three groups evenly, to avoid any confrontations that are likely to occur. Near the end of the session, each group will need to divide in half again. It is possible to plan this in advance, in order to ensure continuity of the session, and a pro forma at the back of the book assists in this task.

The session aims to lead the children in an effective brainstorming session to provide an advertising campaign for an ailing zoo, so some work prior to the session regarding advertisements would benefit the post-session work quality.

THE SESSION

"Welcome to you all. You have been called in by the Board of Directors for Chopper Zoo to support a current crisis, which might eventually close us down. We have realised that we are lacking in two main areas; awareness of what the Zoo does, and money made from ticket sales."

So begins the session. Grouping the children from the outset will help in the organisation of the session. Due to the challenge that awareness may bring for younger children, it might be worth considering just having increased revenue as a focus.

"We realise that we should have asked you to bring an example of some of your previous work today, but we forgot. To help us get to know you better, could you quickly design a poster for a new type of toothpaste, complete with catchphrase?"

The fictitious product and language of this statement can be adjusted according to the group. Other products have previously included jumpers that play CD's and wigs for footballers! Generally, the more unusual, the better.

Give each group about five minutes to produce their poster. This activity introduces them to the idea of putting something in a positive light, and will also allow the teacher to establish the dynamics of each team. If there is a free-for-all discussion, it might be helpful to introduce a conch, which allows only one person to speak at a time, when they are holding the chosen object.

When the five minutes is up, get each group to quickly talk through their posters, justifying their ideas to the other groups. Praise each poster as much as possible. This makes the children see their work as being more valid than the race it can often seem to be.

After this, ask the children to brainstorm positive words or phrases, with each group working on a different topic. Suggested topics are; Images, Opinions and Zoos In General, although these can be tailored to each group. Encourage the children to scribe these as spider charts, with the theme in the middle and all ideas coming outward from it.

When this is complete, display all three sheets, and get a spokesperson from each group to quickly run through the ideas. Ask the class as a whole what the most important three elements from each brainstorm are, and highlight these in some way. This focuses the thoughts of the children, while not dismissing other ideas out of hand.

"We really like your ideas so far, but it's probably best if we explain a little more about the problem that we're experiencing at Chopper Zoo. In short, the number of people visiting us every year is falling, which means we have less money to support all the animals. It has nothing to do with the zoo itself, or the cost of the tickets, just that people don't go to Zoos like they used to."

"One problem we've realised is that the general public don't seem to know about us anymore. They don't know about our conservation campaigns, or new rare species. We want an advertising campaign that relaunches us, to make the public want to come to Chopper Zoo again. Can you think of any ways we could advertise this?"

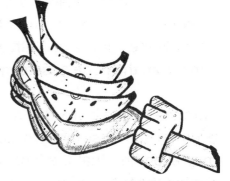

Again, this narration could be shortened or adapted according to the ability of the children, but the essence should remain the same - the need for more customers!

The second part of the speech asks the children for ideas for the advertising campaign. Although they will be creatively exciting, the focus here is for what is actually produced. This has a direct bearing on the end writing result, so don't let the children get carried away. Some suggestions include:

Single sheet
- leaflets, coupons, posters, fliers, sponsorship slips

Multiple sheet
- gatefold leaflets, brochures, information packs, booklets, pages of advertising in a local paper or magazine

Multimedia
- PowerPoint presentation, TV advert, radio advert, website, display stand

Assign one of these to each of the groups. It is wise not to have just one group working on a Multimedia advertisement, since the others will get jealous!

Explain to all groups that their task is to produce an advert (or series of adverts, depending on time restrictions), using the words, phrases and themes identified, for Chopper Zoo.

Use the remaining time in the session for each group to plan their advertisements. At a suitable moment, split each group into two, to ensure that every child is involved in the process. This equates to one advert being made by five children. The teacher could of course divide the class into smaller groups, but the suggested size helps the group to be self-sufficient without being dominated or passive.

FOLLOWING UP

Of all the drama sessions outlined in this book, this particular one has a huge potential for exciting and dynamic work from the children. With an effective free reign on their designs, they often come up with ingenious, and quite different, ways of working towards the same aim. With an inherent love of all things colourful, the adverts usually jump from the page or screen, which is excellent for display work, or for presentations.

With the theme in mind, it might be an option to run the sessions as a competition, or even for the best three to be displayed in the local pet shop or library. The teacher may even find that the local paper wants to be in on the action too - it is worthwhile ringing them to find out if this is so.

The theme of zoos was chosen originally because of the emotive feelings that primary children displayed for animals in general. The theme could easily be adapted to a more appropriate one, from a skate park to a recreation ground. It would not take much to tweak the work, adapting it to the teacher's theme.

CHAPTER NINE

Factory Folk

CONCEPT & AIMS

The children are families during the industrial revolution, suffering all the strain and indignities that went with that lifestyle. They are at a critical stage in their lives, and the scene they act out reflects this.

This is a short session, designed to give a small input that can be explored more thoroughly in the follow-up. The children work on and develop a small scene, on a given or chosen theme, then work to produce a script of that scene.

This session can last from 30 to 60 minutes, depending on the teacher. One alternative is to spend 30 minutes initially, then work on the writing, and finish with another 30 minutes of performance. This is explained more clearly at the end of the chapter.

A group of any size up to 30 can participate in this session.

VENUE AND EQUIPMENT

For the drama, a school hall or empty classroom is best. The children may want to make notes at the end, but this can be done on the floor. The post-session writing can also take place in the hall if preferred.

No equipment is needed, although the children may need any notebooks that they use, and a pencil.

BACKGROUND

This drama requires the children to write a short script about a family in the industrial revolution. Due to this aim, some previous work on scripting and/or that period would be beneficial, although not essential.

Each child will be part of a family during these times, and will be given a situation to play, then script. For time purposes, these are better prepared beforehand, then read to the class at the appropriate moment. To aid the children's imagination, short punchy topics are most suitable. They offer an ambiguity that the children can adapt easily according to their combined abilities. Some suggestions include:

- The Fire, Father Missing, Lost Money, Strange Illness, The Boss, Missing Food

After the sessions, the children are quite adept at offering others to use in future moments. Information on the various stages of writing a script can be found later in the chapter.

THE SESSION

It is best to begin with a story or description of the typical situation of most people during the Industrial Revolution. Emphasise the difficult lifestyle, dangerous working conditions and the lack of an escape route for the majority of people. Be specific about the role of family in those times, and how children were expected to work just as hard as adults, but for less pay.

Divide the children into small groups, and ask them to become a machine, the noisier, dirtier and heavier, the better. Ask for pistons, teeth, wheels and crushing motions. Allow about three minutes for this, then have each group demonstrate their machine to the rest one-by-one, then altogether (it is best to shut the hall doors firmly at this point!). If the session is going to be longer than 30 minutes, ask one or two of the children to work on one of the machines. This produces a good image for both that particular child, and the rest of the group.

In their machine groups (and it is suggested that each group numbers no more than five), ask them to decide which member of the family they choose to be. Encourage the fact that extended families might live together, and grandparents were rare then. Ask them to come up with a short scene to show the rest of the class, depicting their family. This should only take around five minutes to practise, and five to perform.

Give out the slips of paper with the mini-themes on them, and ask the family groups to develop their scene, using their specific theme. Allow a slightly longer time for this, and ensure that each group has an opportunity to demonstrate their scene, which shouldn't take too long to perform.

After each performance, congratulate not just brevity, but good dialogue and an effective use of the theme in their scene. At the end of the session, allow the children a few minutes to make notes on their scene.

WRITING SCRIPTS

This session is very specific in its follow-up writing, in that the children are asked to write a script of their scene performed earlier. Many children will immediately worry that they will forget what actually happened before. What previously occurred is not essential, as they need to develop, rather than reproduce, the scene as writers.

There is an effective way of writing a script with children, and it is built up in clear stages. It is up to the teacher whether to teach each element a stage at a time, or introduce all of the stages and launch the writing task, but the former offers better writing value in the long term.

Character

The children write down all the characters in their scene by name, then write down three physical traits, and three personality traits for each. By limiting the description to six elements, this avoids extended essays on one character that is liked, and one line on those who aren't!

Capturing the scene

The children write down what happens in one sentence. This should be referred to at every following stage, and should be seen as the target for each additional line of dialogue or action. Examples include:

> *"Father comes home and finds his youngest child missing"*
> *"The boss has caught the children stealing from the shop"*
> *"Mother is very ill in bed with an unknown illness"*

Monologuing

This is quite a difficult skill with writing, but in essence is like a police statement, or a sports commentary. The children choose one of the characters previously described, and get that character to describe the entire scene from their point of view. This offers the children a chance to practise speaking in another voice, and also offers some potential soundbites for their script at a later stage. This can be any length, but is best written in pencil. Some children like to underline small extracts or phrases from this for future reference, which is very helpful for their writing.

Dialoguing

This stage asks the children to write down all the conversation that occurs in the scene. The most effective way to do this is to assign a small code for each character (M for mother, and so on), then write out phrases that each character may say in the scene.

Some children prefer to write down the scene as prose, then break it into separate lines afterwards. This is quite long winded, and it is suggested that these children write on lined paper, then cut up the separate lines, reordering and gluing them onto a new sheet.

All of the dialoguing should be done leaving a gap between each line, in order to make space for future inclusions and changes.

Expressions

Even the most competent playwrights give their characters expressive cues, in order to focus the direction of the line, and this skill is very beneficial for the children's work on verbs and adverbs. To show how important offering an expression for the dialogue is, examine the following lines:

(Angrily)   **How did they find out?**
(Sadly)   **How did they find out?**
(Slowly and quietly) **How did they find out?**
(Rapidly)   **How did they find out?**

Children take to writing the expression cues quite quickly, and tend to smother all of the lines with as many terms of expression as possible. Some restraint is needed sometimes - over-expressive scripts become farces!

Stage directions

Moving a character about in a script is an additional thing for the actor to do, but helps the writer to make sure the actors do what they're supposed to! The children need to find a balance between static characters, and those who seem to be running a marathon, whilst juggling all the props possible!

For larger scenes, some children have preferred to choreograph their character's movements using counters on a plan of their stage set. This clearly indicates when and where a character should be in the scene, but can be quite time-consuming, so is better for longer sessions.

Proofing

Often the most difficult stage, the children should read their finished script aloud, listening to their dialogue. Is it convincing, or difficult to say, or even too poetic? This is a very hard skill to develop, so some teachers may prefer to move straight to the next stage, which does the equivalent, but in a different way.

Public Reading ▨▨▨▨▨▨▨▨▨▨▨▨▨▨▨▨▨▨▨▨▨▨▨▨▨▨▨▨▨▨▨▨▨▨▨▨▨▨

This gives each child an opportunity to hear their finished script being read by separate characters. This can be done as a small group, or in front of the whole class, although the latter can take an awfully long time to carry out.

It is best for each child in the reading to have a copy of the script, rather than share the original. It is also better for each character to read over their lines before the performance, as this eliminates some of the pausing at an illegible or challenging word.

FOLLOWING UP

The most obvious way of following up the scriptwriting and drama is to perform them, but this can be done in a number of ways. The most conventional way is for the children to act each other's script out. It is important to spend at least half of this time listening to feedback from the others about the script. Areas of development as well as good elements should be discussed, although the writer will usually have identified this from the performance itself.

Radio plays and short films are also suitable forms of following up the script work, and provide a lasting reminder of the event for the children. The collated scripts also make an excellent anthology for the class and teacher.

This period in history was chosen originally because of a need for more humanities work, but the session could easily be adapted into another environment - the scriptwriting stage remains the same. There is great potential for humorous writing with this type of activity, and this is an area that could be explored in the future.

The work that is produced with scriptwriting is often so impressive, it becomes frustrating for the teacher that work of this calibre is not produced during creative prose. One way to tackle this difficulty is to translate one to the other; from script to prose or vice versa. This activity highlights the role of dialogue in dictating a story descriptively, and also adds an editorial element to the children's writing that they might not normally be used to.

CHAPTER TEN

War Warriors

CONCEPT & AIMS

The children are a tired band of soldiers/civilians, returning home after a long and damaging battle.

This session is short, and aims to inspire thoughts and feelings in the children that would be most appropriate for war poetry. Any event such as a violent conflict can create a situation of unity within a group, as well as a personal isolation, and this session aims to be no exception to this empathy.

War Warriors should last no longer than thirty minutes, without serious commitment to the topic in hand. Any size of group is possible with this session, although it is more appropriate to organise this for older children.

VENUE AND EQUIPMENT

A hall is ideal for the session, as space is used to great effect later in the drama.

A skipping rope, several beanbags and blindfolds for every child are needed for this session, although alternatives may spring to mind (for example, a broom handle instead of skipping rope).

Some carefully chosen war poetry is needed at the end of the session. This is readily available, and is often quite powerful and touching. Ensure that the passages are appropriate for the age-group, and make some copies for afterwards.

BACKGROUND

As a short input, drama can often have quite an impact on the following work. A simple imagined conversation can support some dialogue work, and hot-seating or role-play can offer the children a snapshot of the aims, without unnecessary study or worksheets.

Similarly, this session can be used "as is", but should also be treated as a model for ways to convey a point that might almost be too hard to otherwise get across. The session takes little time, allowing the children participating to involve themselves in the nuts and bolts of their work more quickly.

It is built on team activities that have a bias towards defeat and group failure. The experience of a battle is then transferred onto the children subtly. It is stated that the children could be either soldiers or citizens - this is up to the discretion of the teacher in charge. Experience has shown that a mixture of the two works well, but choosing one in particular has a more empathetic effect with the group.

The main challenge with this session is that some rules that you may give will possibly need to be adjusted or bent to suit the result of the activity. It should be remembered that the group must fail some of the activities.

STAGES

1. Minefield ██

The children should blindfold each other tightly, and set them a task of finding a space of their own on the hall floor. When the children have adjusted and are quiet, explain that one child is going to remove their blindfold, and as quietly as possible, tap each child on the head.

The rest of the group has to listen carefully for any movements. If they hear anything, they must cover their ears - this means they can't be tapped. Play this game several times.

This game adjusts the children to the dark, and temporarily focuses their attentions of the sounds around them.

2. Come Together ████████████████████████████████████

Still with blindfolds, explain that one child will be given a length of rope, and the others must try to join as quickly as possible to the rope by holding onto it, in order to survive. They aren't allowed to make any sounds to do this. Play this several times, each time making the time limit shorter and shorter.

On the last turn of the game, the teacher holds back the rope, but says it has been distributed. Observe the group's efforts to locate the rope, and then their frustration at being tricked.

This game aims to make the group work together under the most difficult of circumstances to achieve a goal. It could be worth a small discussion of their feelings at being duped if the atmosphere is not placated.

3. The Start of the Walk

Have the children walk around in random patterns, and after a while, ask them to drift slowly into a line, following a chosen child. Slow the speed of the first child down (forcing the others to follow suit), and form a sitting circle on the floor.

Discuss how it felt to rely on their hearing alone for the first exercise, or the betrayal they felt in the second. Ask for their views of the third task. A walk without a purpose is more difficult to describe than one with a purpose. In a war situation, what could that walk be to, or from? What could it symbolise? Discuss these with the children, making notes if appropriate.

4. Examples

In the same position as before, read some of the prepared war poetry, asking the children to listen out for a phrase that strikes a chord with them. If time is not a factor, it might be possible to ask the children to create a tableau (3D photograph) of the phrase.

In this reflective state, ask the children to clear their minds, and picture just one moment of a situation like those they had heard. Ask them to add all the details; from colours and objects, to senses and feelings. Ask them to move around in their mind and explore their scene more fully. If possible, get one or two individuals to describe their scene for the others.

When all images have been formed and described adequately, return to the classroom for the writing element of the session. This can alternatively take place in the hall itself.

FOLLOWING UP

This session is very specific about its final outcomes - war poetry. There are, of course, other avenues that can be explored further in this way, but the intention is that the experience would prompt a better response in the children's writing. War poetry is very focused in its style and content, which helps when offering children a model to work from. Other forms of poetry could work just as well when examined with the possibility of drama attached.

Where the ideas can diverge is with the presentation of the work. Poetry is, by its very nature, physically quite narrow, and many images or silhouettes can be made in a narrow form, as a backdrop to the poems. Likewise, recognisable images of war such as gas masks or Spitfires are exceptionally effective ways to add something to the presentation of the poems. Creating an anthology of the class's work is beneficial for the group in question, and for future classes.

SECTION TWO

Preparing
Drama Sessions

CHAPTER ELEVEN

Surviving a Drama Session

As suggested earlier in the introduction, many teachers are put off trying drama in their classes out of genuine concerns. These concerns can range from the actual educational value of drama, of the unpredictability of drama, or simply due to the group of children they have. There are countless strategies for tackling each of these issues, and this chapter merely highlights some strategies and arguments that have been used successfully in the past.

HOW CAN DRAMA BE EDUCATIONAL?

The purpose of drama in the context of this book is as a way of stimulating creative writing. Treating the drama as an educational tool can ease the teacher's conscience much better. Many lessons involve studying artefacts, or researching lives and situations to discover or learn more about them, and drama works in much the same way, except that the children are using their own experiences as the resources, rather than any objects or resources the teacher has prepared. As a result of this, there is far more ownership to what is discovered, since it is an absolute truth to the child involved. In any good mathematics lesson, the teacher would relate the static maths concepts into something real for the children, and using drama for creative writing is doing the same thing but in reverse. By living different experiences and feelings, drama can help the child to better explain them in their speech and writing.

In a small-scale study by the author, drama was found to have a deeper impression on a child's long-term memory than conventional teaching methods. An imaginary history topic was taught in two ways, traditionally and using drama only, and post-lesson tests long after the event showed that those children who had experienced the drama teaching had far better recall of the story than those who had learned under more traditional methods.

This is not to say that drama should be used every time. If treated as a resource, then its use must suit the task. Just as a teacher may not use worksheets or an overhead projector each lesson, constant use of drama can eventually be wearing and dull for both the teacher and the class.

ISN'T DRAMA TOO UNPREDICTABLE?

Only if it is allowed to be. A carefully planned and executed drama session gives little opportunity to become unpredictable. Many of the drama sessions in this book are broken down into stages, specifically to direct the narration of the story. Any event that has no end goal or direction has every opportunity to be unpredictable.

There are times when an unpredictable situation is exciting for both the class and the leading teacher, but it is suggested that you offer choice with direction. If you are to fulfil the aim of the drama session, you must have some idea of the direction the drama should head for, so offer a range of choices, all of which are compatible with achieving your aim.

One of the most famous of drama practitioners, Dorothy Heathcote, was a strong advocate of child-led drama, where the class chose the time, events and direction of the drama. Her role was one of passive control, whilst subtly introducing the conflicts that make any drama come alive. Her books and videos are quite inspirational, but it takes years of development to have the confidence and courage to tackle anything like the drama Dorothy Heathcote initiated.

Since the aim of drama here is to stimulate creative writing, it is suggested that her style of drama is only tried when very confident, and when the pressures of the curriculum are lessened.

WHAT IF THE CHILDREN GET TOO EXCITED?

The basis of any drama is to introduce a conflict and then attempt to resolve it. The children becoming excited demonstrates that perhaps the conflict is not strong enough for that group of children. If this excitement is beginning to become apparent, the teacher must quickly increase the level of conflict. If possible, stun the children into silence. Indicate that for whatever reason, they have all let the group down. Any additional pressure applied to the children will quickly refocus their energies into solving the dilemma they find their characters in.

There are occasions when excitement is welcome, encouraged even. Always allow an escape clause, in order to reduce the excitement levels if they increase beyond an acceptable amount. One example of this is in 'The Paper Aeroplane', where the final stage is when the children put on a circus display. If the children become too involved, it is possible to warn the children of an accident by one of the acrobats, and that they had better be more careful in their performance.

It must be remembered that the group are just children, and excitement is a sign of enjoyment. By pinpointing what is making the children excited, different approaches can quickly be thought of to make this excitement more controlled.

WHAT ABOUT MY REALLY GOOD ACTORS?

The most important aspect of the drama sessions described in this book is that children should experience something to help their writing. There are many opportunities for performance and rehearsed drama within the life of a school, but these sessions shouldn't be viewed as a platform for polished performance. If this becomes apparent to the children, then those with less dramatic ability will start comparisons, and their enthusiasm and participation will wane considerably.

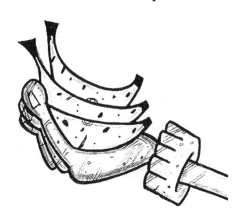

It is not possible of course to even out the dramatic talent of a class; some children are naturally better at creating imagined situations than others. This situation can be of great benefit to others in demonstrating something, just as long as a demonstration doesn't become a performance. Drama sessions of this nature often allow children who you wouldn't normally expect to do well, to shine.

Try and avoid judging the various dramatic talents of the children during a session; remember, the most crucial aspect is what the children take from the drama, not how much applause they get.

MY CLASS JUST WOULDN'T COPE WITH THIS!

There are undoubtedly many "untouchable" classes, probably one in every school. These are the classes that teachers breathe a sigh of relief when discovering that they aren't teaching them. That is not to say that they will react badly to drama sessions in the way you might normally expect. If a group is driven by a collective purpose, drama can actually benefit them, by making them acutely aware of individual actions having a collective reaction.

The teachers of this type of class are most likely well aware of the class's abilities and foibles in different situations. When planning a drama session, these factors need to be taken into account. Are there situations it would be uncomfortable to enter into, or are they too cynical to fully immerse in some of the situations described?

When choosing or creating a drama session, these abilities need to be taken into account, and plundered as much as possible. In many cases, a positive response to something different can minutely adjust the class ethos to trying something new. While it must be remembered that these sessions are not a panacea for creative writing difficulties, they can help in many other ways.

I HAVE THIS ONE CHILD . . .

With inclusion being such an important issue in today's education system, there are still some children who have the ability to upset the whole balance of a class, and can prove to be high-maintenance pupils as far as their teacher is concerned. As with a challenging class, challenging pupils need as much positive channelling as possible. When planning a session, the teacher should consider what could go wrong with this child in the given situation, and decide on suitable courses of action to prevent any possible difficulties.

Developing an unspoken sense of hierarchy and status can help this situation. Asking the individual to play a vital and important role (that the teacher has predetermined) in the drama may help to avoid a more obvious, more disruptive, role that the child might otherwise have chosen.

Likewise, there may be one or two children who are quite nervous in group or spotlight situations; they too must be included as much as possible. Ensuring that they are one of a group of characters can help to begin with, since this takes an immediate focus from them. Gradually, they can be drawn away from the group to more of an individual role. Generally, there is usually so much going on at once in a session that many inhibitions are simply forgotten over time.

CAN I JUSTIFY THE TIME COST?

Each drama session lasts around an hour, with a few exceptions. Add to this a writing session and an evaluation, and you have three hours to justify.

The best way to do this is to consider the benefits that one session can bring to the writing. The teacher could very well carry out three consecutive lessons on a specific written development and achieve nothing at all. Balance this against the sessions detailed, where the children experience, write and evaluate in the same time. Trying a drama session once may help to justify what at first might seem like an extravagant length of time. It is often better to spend more time on something that the child understands, than to stop due to time constraints, and leave learning incomplete.

I DON'T LIKE DRAMA MYSELF!

None of the prescribed sessions require the teacher to act in any way. Many of them use the numerous skills of storytelling, organising and concept development that teachers use in teaching other curriculum areas anyway. Despite the difference in activity for the children, the teacher's role remains largely unchanged - if chosen. There are many opportunities for the teacher to become much more deeply involved than the sessions describe - but this is entirely up to the teacher in question.

The pleasure that the children take from their work during and after a drama session will hopefully help to improve the teacher's perception of drama in schools. It is fully understandable that teachers will prefer teaching some subjects to others, but this can be countered with the pleasure received when the children proudly recognise their achievements in the drama and subsequent writing.

CHAPTER TWELVE

Warm-up Games

Warm up games are not necessary, or needed, for any drama sessions in this book. They do however have many benefits for the children in various forms. The children may display more enthusiasm sometimes for the games than for the main activity - but don't be misled. If the intention at the session is for creative writing, not much will come about through drama only.

Opening games can be used to highlight or define, or even hone, a particular skill you wish to make the children aware of. They are also good at focussing the children to a different type of working. They are effective as bonding activities, or even cooling down activities. Some of the games featured are not particularly drama-driven, but they are fun nevertheless!

The games are either total participation, or involve only one or two children at a time. If you are planning to play two games (each of those below only take about five minutes each), it is best to begin with one where all the children are involved, then the next can be for individuals to "shine".

BEANBAGGER

Objective: concentration skills, recall, focus ▨ ▨ ▨ ▨ ▨ ▨ ▨ ▨ ▨ ▨ ▨ ▨ ▨ ▨ ▨ ▨ ▨ ▨ ▨

This game is very exciting and fun for all, but does require a very high level of concentration from the children, making it only suitable for junior aged children.

The children sit in a circle on the floor, with their hands up. The leader passes a beanbag to one person, whilst saying their name, this person catches it, puts their hand down, and passes it to another player. When all children have caught the beanbag once, it should end up with the leader. This is when the fun starts! Start the passing again, with the children passing to those that they passed to before. Do this several times, encouraging them to get faster.

There are several variations that you can add to this. It is possible to send the beanbag backwards (pass the beanbag to the person who originally passed it to you), you could introduce more beanbags, or even time a complete circuit.

The children could try passing in silence, or changing positions at a command, then continuing the game. This last suggestion really keeps the children on their toes! Once all these variations have been tried out, ask the children to come up with more.

ALL CHANGE

Objective: listening skills, dexterity, targeting ▨▨▨▨▨▨▨▨▨▨▨▨▨▨▨▨

All children bar one sit in a circle of chairs. The child decides a category, and all those that fit that category have to change seats with someone else. Anyone left without a seat becomes the person left in the middle. Categories include; all those with white socks on, all those with blue eyes, all those who eat cornflakes, all those with a pet dog.

At any point, a child can call out "All Change," and all the children have to change.

COPYCAT

Objective: study skills, copying, motor skills, distracting ▨▨▨▨▨▨▨▨▨▨▨▨

The children sit in a circle, with one child outside the room. The leader chooses one child to begin a repetitive action that the rest of the group has to copy. This can be patting their head, slow clapping, chicken impressions. The person outside comes in and has three guesses to discover who the leader is.

The tendency of the children is to watch the leader intently at first. Explain that this gives the game away, and ask them to find some other way of finding out what the current action is.

JOIN-UP

Objective: concentration, lateral thinking, linking concepts ▨▨▨▨▨▨▨▨▨▨

The children sit in a circle, and the leader gives the first child a word. The child to the left has to think of a connecting word, and then the child on their left has to think of a new connecting word. One chain might begin:

cheese - knife - fork - spoon - tea - coffee - cup - cake - wedding

If the game-play is too slow, you might suggest a hurrying tactic, such as all those children who can think of a new connecting word pat the floor quickly. This can quickly spur on those who are intentionally dawdling.

BRANTUB

Objective: writing skills, listening, altering ideas

Give the children a theme (the circus, woods, a castle), and ask the children to write four poetic lines on four small pieces of paper. Put all these into a tin, and then have each child draw four out randomly.

The children can then adjust the lines according to their taste, or edit them as they choose. Many children love this activity as an opening activity for writing poetry, since it often gives them a kick-start on a poem.

AWARDS

Objectives: improvisation, creative thinking

On three separate slips of paper, each child writes their name, a fun "stage name" and a strange award. Collect these up in three containers (labelled jam jars are ideal for this), and then select one from each.

The name is the person presenting the strange award to the strange name. Some examples include; Princess Balletshoes winning the Longest Yawn Award, Jumping John receiving the Award for Smelliest Shoes and Diceman winning the Looks-like-a-Frog Award.

The winner makes a small, but appropriate, speech. Underline the fact that the awards must be fun and strange, but never personal.

ADVERBIALLY

Objective: miming, accuracy, understanding of adverbs

One child leaves the room, and one of those left chooses an adverb (e.g. strangely, madly, tiredly, slowly). The chosen child then returns to the room, and asks someone to mime an action like walking a dog or reading a book. That child then performs the action in the style of the adverb.

BORING MUSEUM

Objectives: improvisation, creative thinking ▧ ▧ ▧ ▧ ▧ ▧ ▧ ▧ ▧ ▧ ▧ ▧ ▧ ▧ ▧ ▧ ▧ ▧ ▧

Take one child aside, and decide on a very boring museum exhibition, like "Spoons of the World" or "Dangerous Washing Machines". The child then provides either an introduction or a mini tour of the exhibit for a minute or two. The rest of the children then have to guess what the exhibition is about.

It is best to choose children with a lot of confidence at first, to get them in the swing of things. After a while, the teacher will be swamped with volunteers.

MIRRORING

Objectives: concentration, copying, reflex responses ▧ ▧ ▧ ▧ ▧ ▧ ▧ ▧ ▧ ▧ ▧ ▧ ▧

The children stand about a foot apart from each other in pairs, and imagine that there is a mirror between them. They number themselves one and two, and become either the leader or the reflection. Ask the leaders to perform a mundane task such as getting dressed or brushing teeth, and the reflections have to copy their actions as best as they can.

After a while, swap the action and the leader, so that each child gets a turn.

NEW ARMS

Objectives: quick thinking, dexterity ▧

In pairs, one child stands behind the other and puts their arms under those in front. Ask them to perform a task as best they can, like preparing and eating breakfast.

Walk around observing the actions, and tap on the shoulder those pairs whose performance is unconvincing. The last pair standing wins.

HUNT THE KEY

Objectives: listening skills, stealth, delicate movements ▨ ▨ ▨ ▨ ▨ ▨ ▨ ▨ ▨ ▨ ▨ ▨

The children sit in a circle, with a chair in the middle. Have one child blindfold and sitting in the chair, with a large bunch of keys on the floor behind them. Point at an individual, and they must then retrieve the keys and sit back down. The blindfolded child on the chair has three chances to point at where the sound is coming from.

If the child gets the keys successfully, they then sit on the chair.

RING LEADERS

Objectives: observation, deception, co-operation ▨ ▨ ▨ ▨ ▨ ▨ ▨ ▨ ▨ ▨ ▨ ▨ ▨ ▨ ▨

Get a length of string as large as the circle of children, and make it into a loop, with a ring on it. Ask one child to stand out, then move the ring to a set point.

All the children put their hands on the string, and pretend to, or genuinely pass the ring from hand to hand. The chosen child has three chances to guess where the ring is. At a guess, those who have been pointed to have to reveal whether or not they have the ring.

ENDING UP

Objectives: convincing stories, quick thinking ▨ ▨ ▨ ▨ ▨ ▨ ▨ ▨ ▨ ▨ ▨ ▨ ▨ ▨ ▨

Get each child to write down a difficult ending line to a story, that begins, "which is how I ended up..." Examples include;

- *"President of the United States"*
- *"Having a gorilla staying at my house"*
- *"Robbing a bank with my gran"*

Choosing one child at a time, let them choose a statement at random, give them a short time to read it over and think, then begin a minute timer for the child to make up a story on the spot which ends with the line chosen.

WAIT A MINUTE

Objectives: concentration, timing ▨ ▨ ▨ ▨ ▨ ▨ ▨ ▨ ▨ ▨ ▨ ▨ ▨ ▨ ▨ ▨ ▨ ▨ ▨

This is a very short game that is excellent for calming and quietening a group of children down immediately. Sitting at their tables, ask the children to fold their arms on the top and rest their heads, closing their eyes. Tell them to sit up when they think that a minute is up. Tell them when the minute starts. The winner is the person who sits up closest to a minute.

PARTY GUESTS

Objectives: impersonation, acting skills ■

An old favourite, ask one person (the host) to leave the room, then choose four children to decide on a particular trait (they are invisible, the best dancer in the world, think they are a cat etc.), then ask the host in.

They then invite each guest in, in turn, and must guess their particular trait. It might be helpful for more difficult traits to offer the host clues.

REMOVAL FIRM

Objectives: special awareness, miming, co-operation ■ ■ ■ ■ ■ ■ ■ ■ ■ ■ ■ ■ ■

This game can be played either as a group together or as a pair performing to the others, as is described below.

The pair decides on a particularly unusual object to remove. They can carry, wrap, push, lift or move it in any way to offer clues to what it is. The watching children have to guess what the object is, and those that guess correctly have the next turn. Good starting objects include; a stuffed moose, a large piano, the Statue of Liberty, a greasy cheese sandwich.

CHAT SHOW

Objectives: improvising, offering clues ■

Choose one child to be the chat show host, and ask them to leave the room. Choose three guests, and decide on who they are or what they do. The more outlandish jobs, the better the game. One of the best seen was an elephant manicurist!

The host interviews each guest in turn, trying to find out what the person actually does. Some of their questions can be quite unintentionally funny, or dangerously perceptive.

ANIMAL OLYMPICS

Objectives: mime, concentration, interpreting actions ▨▨▨▨▨▨▨▨▨▨▨▨▨▨

In small groups, decide on an unusual sport at the Animal Olympics. This can be as diverse as the Shark Javelin, Giraffe Synchronised Swimming or even Tortoise Table-tennis. As each group performs silently, the others must guess both the animal and the sport.

THE BEST OF THE WORST

Objectives: creative thinking, copying, prediction ▨▨▨▨▨▨▨▨▨▨▨▨▨▨

This is an exhausting but very funny game to play. Choose a child as an expert in something, and get them to lead a workshop or demonstration in their specialisation. They are officially the worst at this, but think they are the best. Some good subjects include dance teachers, pottery makers, chefs.

The rest of the children must carry out whatever instructions are given as best they can, without giving away the fact that the leader is appaling. If the teacher is brave enough, it is often best if they give the first demonstration, in order to show how bad to be!

VERY, VERY, VERY . . .

Objectives: exaggeration, miming, developing actions ▨▨▨▨▨▨▨▨▨▨▨▨▨

The children can all participate in this game if there is enough space for them all. Choose a simple, normal action, which can be as mundane as reading or walking or even sleeping. Instruct the children to increase their mime - from "tired" they must be "very tired", then "very, very tired". Continue this to the children's exhaustion.

BOMB DISPOSAL

In pairs, explain that there is a bomb that needs diffusing in front of them. Underline the fact that this needs to be done as carefully and delicately as possible. The teacher provides the instructions. One set of instructions might be;

"There are three wires on the bottom of the bomb. Carefully cut the red wire. Now cut the yellow wire. Take one end of the red wire, and one end of the yellow, and slowly twist them together . . . "

Such is the concentration given by the children for this game, it can last for up to ten minutes. Depending on the ability of the children, the teacher could set them off on diffusing a similar bomb on their own, each person in the pair offering instructions to the other, then swapping over.

68

CHAPTER THIRTEEN

Follow-up Sessions

Although all of the sessions detailed in this book can be used in isolation, many of them have great scope for follow-up sessions. The first question that should be asked is why follow them up? Perhaps it was the quality of the drama that was shown, or the standard of the writing that occurred afterwards. Either way, there must be a specific reason for continuing the work, otherwise it might appear to be directionless to both you and the children

FOLLOWING UP THE DRAMA

Any good drama session will leave questions unanswered. For much of the time, this is an advantage for the teacher, since the children have a chance to direct proceedings in their writing, or even to answer the questions themselves in their writing. On other occasions, the unanswered areas are too intriguing to be left alone. It is important to give some thought to what you want to achieve when continuing a drama session, and what benefit it will bring, and it is strongly recommended that you don't try to tie up all the loose ends. This gives a very concrete finish to the drama, and may curtail any future drama sessions.

It is worth writing down some notes to support a follow-up session involving drama, if only to give you some feeling of control over events. Answering the following questions may help you in this task:

- What was unresolved at the last session?
- What would you like to occur in this session?
- Are there any areas to explore?
- Are there any areas to avoid?
- How do you want this session to end?
- How will you go about achieving this?
- What will be unresolved at the end of this session?
- How will this session support the children's creative writing?
- What ways do you want the children to record the events of this session?

A follow-up form featuring these questions is in the back of the book. One area of particular note are the areas you wish to avoid. Some situations that can spontaneously occur in a drama session, such as suffering or loyalty, are sometimes more suited to a PHSE lesson or class discussion. Any situation that puts a child's emotions in conflict or even harm should be avoided at all costs. You are trying to inspire creative writing, not attempting child-therapy.

Other considerations should go to whether you are trying to extend the drama, or the range of creative writing. Is an additional session suitable for this, or is it just drama for drama's sake? Very often, some additional work with the creative writing aspect can more than compensate for your concerns.

FOLLOWING UP THE WRITING

Just one session of drama can yield many sessions of creative writing on the drama. Children however get tired very quickly of simply rehashing the same work, and this should be avoided. The best position to be in is to stop the children as close to mid-flow as possible – thus holding their enthusiasm. One format for the use of drama sessions can be seen as a three-stage approach:

Stage One: The Drama ▧▧▧▧▧▧▧▧▧▧▧▧▧▧▧▧▧▧▧▧▧▧▧▧▧▧▧▧▧▧▧▧▧▧▧▧▧▧

This is a session devoted to the drama itself, and can often not involve any writing at all, although it may be worth either you or the children recording key situations or events. It might also be worth taking pictures or recordings, to help with the continuing stages.

Stage Two: The Writing ▧▧

This can be carried out in one discreet session, or spread out over a week in ten-minute slots (using a diary approach). This enables the children to write down their experiences as thoughtfully as possible, and should therefore be done as soon after the drama session as possible – memories fade very quickly, and are practically redundant after a week or so.

Stage Three: Evaluation and Analysis ▧▧▧▧▧▧▧▧▧▧▧▧▧▧▧▧▧▧▧▧▧▧▧▧▧▧▧▧▧▧▧

This is for the benefit of both you and the children. Lasting one session, this is an opportunity to showcase any writing or work done by the children, and to see how it captured a moment/could be improved. Children love reading out their work, and it is well worth pointing out one or two elements that you particularly like for each work – the children will come up with their own suggestions for you!

This is also a chance for you to discuss with the children the value of the drama session, and what effect they thought it had on their writing. They might also like to talk about elements that they didn't like, found hard or simply did not understand.

Whilst this may come across as criticism of you, it gives an excellent idea of how the sessions were viewed and enjoyed by the children. It is rare for a child to find nothing that they liked or improved on.

Assuming that you are the only teacher in your school to have used drama in this way to develop and improve the creative writing of your class, it is worthwhile displaying the work prominently, or even drawing attention to it at a staff meeting. Perhaps others on the staff will catch the drama bug too!

All three stages will take around three hours in total, although there is much scope for adjusting this for a Book Week to five hours. As a rule of thumb, make the time devoted to writing at least equal to the time spent acting, and never cut out the evaluation due to time constraints – this is often the most valuable section for you as a teacher. More guidance for planning a series of sessions can be found in the next chapter.

CHAPTER FOURTEEN

Creating your own, or a series of sessions

If you have time and the facilities to do so, running a series of drama sessions as a way of developing creative writing can be an extremely successful and rewarding task. Careful planning however is essential, if the benefits are to be reaped. This chapter will help you to devise your own sessions and adapt these, or the ready-made sessions in this book, into a series of sessions for your class.

Before you begin, it is worth examining and thinking about all those elements that you cannot dictate. These can be as simple as the venue for the drama, the length of each session, any follow-up work that may fall outside the planned sessions, and the effect on any educational constraints or aims within the times. All of these elements will have an important effect on your planning and execution of the sessions, so they need to be borne in mind as soon as possible.

It is also important to consider why you may choose to have more than one drama session. Is it for your pleasure or the children's? Is there a specific aim to the series; is there a direction you want to take the class, or is it drama for drama's sake? Without a key focus, running the sessions may end up tiresome and unfruitful. There is certainly a place for "free" drama, but if you are going to devote a considerable length of time to it, the sessions need to be driven by a key aim or focus. Perhaps the creative writing in the class is particularly weak, or some children have difficulty in describing or visualising situations that are outside their world. In many cases, running a series of drama sessions can provide a large amount of material that can be referred to many times later in the year – this is a reason rather than an aim.

DESIGNING YOUR OWN SESSION

Hopefully, the sessions already described in this book have inspired you enough to go ahead and create your own. If not, don't panic! Developing your own drama session is actually a very simple process, although it shouldn't be rushed. The best way to do this is backwards, as the model on the next page shows.

What type of writing do you want to produce?

Decide on the eventual outcome of the drama session

How will this be achieved?

What situations would help?

How will you run the session?

Does this cater for the entire group?

Session Planning Model

By answering these questions carefully, it shouldn't take too long to plan a session for the children. A pro forma of these questions can be found at the back of the book, to copy and fill in. The Space Farm session earlier in the book is used for the examples, to help you when planning your own session.

WHAT TYPE OF WRITING DO YOU WANT TO PRODUCE?

If the drama is a means to a (creatively written) end, then your first thought must be the type or style of writing you are aiming to receive from the children at the conclusion of the drama. Is it impersonal or personal, entirely fictional, or based on fact? By examining the writing first, this narrows the choice of drama, thereby focusing you to the most appropriate type of event, place and storylines.

DECIDING ON THE EVENTUAL OUTCOME OF THE DRAMA SESSION

Although it is sometimes very exciting to not know where the drama may go next, it is highly recommended that you decide the eventual outcome of the session. With this in mind, all the interesting tangents can be explored, but not at a cost to the aim of the session. Any alternative avenues may help the children's writing, and may also give opportunities to reach the outcome by a different route.

HOW WILL THIS BE ACHIEVED?

This is probably the most deceptively simple aspect of the planning, but is easily done in stages, working back. If, as an example, your eventual outcome was to see how friends react to torn loyalty, by working backwards, you can register the stages the children need to go through.

Outcome	Stage
How do friends react to torn loyalty?	Introduce conflict
What is a conflict?	Example of conflict – group against x
How strong is the friendship?	Develop team unity through support activity

By looking at the final outcome first, you can see the building blocks needed to ensure you reach that final outcome. The different stages needed to achieve these mini-outcomes form the basis of the different activities you will need to carry out in order to progress.

It is wise to assume nothing unless you know the children exceptionally well. In the above example, the outcome "what is a conflict?" has been included, whether necessary or not. As a result, those who don't know what a conflict is will find out, and those who already know will have their knowledge refreshed.

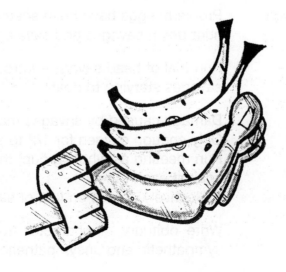

WHAT SITUATIONS WOULD HELP?

This is the opportunity to home in on the actual detail of the session. Although there are some examples of these in Chapter Seventeen (and the children can come up with many more), the key elements are:

- The time
- The place
- The actual location
- The children's roles
- Other roles
- The opening scene

From our example, the topic of torn loyalty is a universal theme, so is free of any time constraints. If you chose to focus on bravery, you would require a situation that could become dangerous, so limiting your choice of situations and events.

HOW WILL YOU RUN THE SESSION?

Once you have decided on all the above, you will need to flesh your ideas out into a tangible drama session. With thought to your situation, create an activity for each of your outcomes. The more specific they are, the more effective they will be. Aim to ensure that each activity fits into the storyline, rather than as a series of unrelated tasks. If the flow of the drama seems seamless and logical, then the writing at the end will more than likely also seem coherent.

Stage	Activity
Introduce location	Using claps, slow movements down. Observe and identify animals on farm
Introduce roles	Check animals for any problems, and repair any damage to perimeter wall
Develop team unity through supportive activity	Problem: eggs have been snatched by savages – hunt down savages and save eggs
Give example of conflict – whole group against x	Run trial of head savage – introduce problem of savages starving to death
Introduce conflict	Damage caused by savages makes farm unsafe. Only enough oxygen for 1/2 to survive. Run meeting as whole group, then pit friendship pairs against each other. Collectively decide on fate of each member
Writing Task	Write obituary of character from two points of view – sympathetic and unsympathetic

DOES THIS CATER FOR THE ENTIRE GROUP?

It is essential that you try, wherever possible, to ensure that each child benefits from the drama. Those who are normally reticent to take charge can be given more prominent roles, and it is also possible to experiment with different friendship circles. Drama can often help the child's social development as well as their creative writing; it should be remembered that this is not your primary aim though.

When you have finished planning your session, try and evaluate it. Is it coherent? Have you allowed enough time for the activities? Where could it go wrong? Do all the activities benefit the final outcome and aims of the session? It may be worthwhile having a colleague examine it, as another person may notice something that had not occurred to you.

It is always helpful to write an evaluation on the other side of your planning after the event. Try and detail any interesting observations or comments, what the children found easy or hard, and what you would change if you were to repeat the drama. It may also be helpful to attach to the planning some copies of the resulting writing, as proof that it really did help!

PLANNING FOR A SERIES OF SESSIONS

If you are confident about planning a whole series, then the planning process is much the same as for an individual session. It is worth examining your time carefully when planning, in order to build up the momentum of the sessions carefully. One session a week over a half term is ideal – this gives you six sessions, and doesn't intrude too much in the other areas of the curriculum.

The basic layout of the six sessions remains the same, whatever the theme. Whilst these can be adjusted according to your time or other constraints, try to keep as close to them as possible. 'The Space Farm' session has again been used as an example to model your own sessions on.

Week	Session
1	Introduction of situation
2	Development of characters
3	Subsidiary situation 1
4	Subsidiary situation 2
5	Final situation
6	Conclusion & development

INTRODUCTION OF SITUATION

This session can be used in acclimatising the children to their location and time. This can be done through description of the location, and the children's own personal discoveries. One way this could be carried out for the 'Space Farm' is for the teacher to introduce a farm tool for the exotic animals, describing it and demonstrating how it works. This could then be repeated by the children and their tools. This helps the children to focus their attentions on the situation, and can of course be used further on in the series.

DEVELOPMENT OF CHARACTERS

Within your chosen situation are many opportunities for roles and jobs for the children, and this session is dedicated to the refinement of these jobs. If you or the children have decided to be children in the 'Space Farm' drama, this session is the ideal chance to build these characters. This could be done by explaining that the children are self-taught, and would be expected to help around the farm with different errands and tasks. The children could then explain the tasks, or demonstrate them. They need to be plausible and realistic in their actions, and remind them of this, in as much of a role as you can muster ("Would you really be expected to take the flying elephants for a ride? They look very dirty – it might be worth helping out by cleaning their wings with this oil.")

This session suits demonstration very well. After all the activities, take time to stop and replay some of the events, so that the rest of the group can see what some individuals do to pass the day. Some hot-seating can also help, then other members of the community can ask questions, or ask to help out next time!

SUBSIDIARY SITUATIONS

These precede the main situation that your overall outcome will draw from. These can be other conflicts or difficulties that the characters will have to survive, and will clearly be of benefit when writing after the sessions.

Simply because they aren't the main focus, don't dismiss this opportunity with trivial events – for a very productive series, you may want more than one aim or outcome, and these subsidiary situations can provide an excellent platform for tackling these. They can of course, build on what has previously occurred, giving cohesion and tension to the drama. The following examples demonstrate these two approaches.

Isolated situations

Week Events

3   Damage in perimeter wall – all characters must help to retrieve as many of the animals as possible, then check each for injury.

4   Food supply cut off – groups must search for other sources of food, then demonstrate how to obtain, cook and eat.
Plant seeds for new food harvest. What is growing?

5   Problem: eggs have been snatched by savages – hunt down savages and save eggs. Introduce problem of savages starving to death.
Farm unsafe. Only enough oxygen for ? to survive. Run meeting as whole group, then pit friendship pairs against each other.

Continued situations

Week Events

3   Problem: eggs have been snatched by savages – hunt down savages and save eggs
How are the eggs treated once retrieved? Do any animals reject the eggs (what then?)

4   Run trial of head savage – introduce problem of savages starving to death
Have some of class 'for', some 'against', and introduce some as witnesses (farmers, savages, animals themselves)

5   Damage caused by savages makes farm unsafe. Only enough oxygen for ? to survive. Run meeting as whole group, then pit friendship pairs against each other. Collectively decide on fate of each member

You will notice that both have the same ending situation, and that the second is merely the 'Space Farm' session spread over three weeks. A lot more detail can go into each stage if you are doing this, for example, swapped roles and a lengthy debate.

Whether you use isolated or continuous situations is dependent on your aims and desired outcome. Sometimes, too many situations can become confusing and hard to keep up with. Conversely, stretching one situation over three weeks can drain it of vitality, and the children of enthusiasm.

CONCLUSION AND DEVELOPMENT

The final session is quite important in rounding up all the events. You may decide not to conclude the story at all and leave it on a plateau – a word of warning. If you have been in the same situation for a number of situations, isn't it fair to share the conclusion with the children? Whilst leaving an isolated session in the air is healthy (advisable even), it is generally more appropriate to return the children to at least normality within their situation. If you were to run the 'Space Farm' series, "discovering" some extra canisters of oxygen would help everyone to survive, and not feel let down after all the effort they had put in during previous sessions.

This is not to suggest that the story couldn't continue. You may wish to use this last session as a chance for the children to discuss further storylines or events that could happen to their characters, or re-enact their best moments again for the others.

This session is an ideal forum for discussion about the story. Are there any elements they disagreed, or even disliked, about their characters? Would they as children have done anything different? How do they feel their character changed or developed over the sessions? One good activity to aid this would be to fast-forward the action several weeks or even years, and recognise the changes. Any children would now be adults, tools and techniques may have changed. Doing this leap of time has little effect on the original outcome, but may help the children to understand or recognise their character a little better.

CHAPTER FIFTEEN

Props

A good prop can help to sustain or develop a drama, and can have a direct effect on the writing produced by the children after a session. Conversely, a badly chosen prop can cause the teacher endless difficulties and hindrances when they are working, and could actually impair the drama by creating problems that could otherwise be avoided.

Because of this, the use and choice of props is more important than might at first be thought. The introduction of props into a drama session isn't advised outside of those prescribed in the sessions outlined in this book until the teacher is confident enough to deal with any difficulties they may entail.

We are all used to handling objects and items in everyday life, and indeed they can enrich conversation, or enhance dialogue. By the same token, props in drama can have the same effect when chosen carefully, and serving a direct purpose. An ordinary music stand was put to excellent use as a makeshift lectern in a past lesson, where the children had to give a talk to the rest of the class. It was used after I realised that the children were more concerned with what to do with their hands and notes, than the content of their talks. As a result, the talks were directed far more at the audience than their nervous palms!

Props have been used in the drama sessions of this book only when absolutely necessary. This was done in order to release the teacher to prepare for the session, rather than rushing around, pleading other colleagues with requests for unusual items. This is not to say that additional props wouldn't be simple to add; quite the opposite.

It is well worth the teacher in charge of Literacy or Drama building up a collection of items that are to be used, or could be put to good use, in future drama sessions. The next couple of pages outline what sort of items can be beneficial as props in drama, and what to keep an eye out for.

TOKENS

Tokens covers a broad spectrum of objects that appeal aesthetically to the children, and can be employed in virtually any drama if needed. Whilst marbles are the classic tokens, previous objects used have ranged from curtain hoops, to buttons, straws and old coins. It is helpful to collect up a set of small ice cream tubs to store the tokens in, perhaps sharing storage space with the Maths equipment (tokens are wonderful for sorting and counting too).

Generally, anything about the size of a key or smaller is ideal as a token. They can be used as coins in an imagined society, hidden treasure, food pellets or seeds, or even take on a mystical presence. In large enough quantities, they are wonderfully tactile props, and the children can handle them quite effectively. If the tokens are going to be used for a series of drama sessions, it may be appropriate to make or find a selection of personal storage pouches or containers for each individual's collection. While empty camera film canisters are excellent for smaller tokens, making cloth pouches is a possibility for larger items. Experience has shown paper containers to be too self-destructing to be reliable!

GYM EQUIPMENT

The 'Rings of Destiny' session that begins the book shows the real potential of using a school's gym equipment in a drama session. It has the advantage of being child-friendly, safe to use and store, and the children will have hopefully received previous experience of handling and using equipment safely.

Large gym equipment lends itself particularly well to creating a physical challenge or obstacle for the children, and can be adapted to suit another purpose extremely quickly.

As with using any potentially dangerous equipment, it is essential to consider the inherent dangers in using gym apparatus, and any necessary permission for using the equipment is obtained. It is advisable not to use gym equipment if it is new or unfamiliar to the children involved in the session. Always ensure that any safety procedures are observed, and use crash-mats if needed. If the teacher is unsure of using the apparatus, it may be helpful to talk over the planned drama with the school's PE specialist, to gain another perspective on usage.

One problem encountered with using gym equipment is the keenness to use every item available, particularly after a promising start. With all the potential dangers involved, it is imperative that each item's use is thoroughly planned for. Impulsive use can quickly open up the opportunity for an accident.

PAPER

One overwhelming delight in children's writing is the opportunity to do something differently. This might be viewed as doing anything to avoid "standard" writing, but couldn't be further from the truth. Children take delight in presenting their work in different styles and formats, and the writing material offered will support this considerably.

A fantastic resource for the writing during or after a drama session is a range of paper to use - the larger the range, the better. Simply having different colours to write on can help develop creative presentation, as can unusual sizes, or shapes of paper. Tea-soaked paper gives a lovely old effect, and burned edges make a map even more authentic, although all sensible routes to achieve this effect should be explored.

Hand-made paper can also have an excellent impression on the writing. This can be produced by using a stick blender to mix together torn squares of computer paper (the continuous pages with punched edges are the best) with a 1:5 mix of PVA glue and water, then sieving through tightly-fixed net curtaining. As part of an Art topic, in time, petals, scents and colours can all add to the quality and finish of the paper.

Likewise, the new "chip" paper can be ordered from educational suppliers, who advertise it as infant painting sheets. This paper is fantastic for newspapers, although ink from bubble-jet printers tends to spread quite quickly, so using a single-feed laser-jet is recommended.

Children often come up with new designs of paper themselves if they are given the opportunity, and this is an area that can be explored more thoroughly in an Art lesson. For younger children, it is more helpful to have a range of prepared papers ready to choose from, or to inspire future ideas.

COSTUMES

I am not an incredibly big fan of costumes, being as restrictive as they are. Introducing costumes into a drama session can cause no end of headaches for the teacher due to the natural competitiveness of the children.

Much more appropriate is a costumed item for a specific role in the drama, the crown for a King being an obvious example. Key items can enhance a role, and also avoid having to dress every child involved.

If the teacher is desperate to use costumes, then it is recommended that they are as non-specific as possible. The most effective use I have seen of this was a large basket of bed-sheet sized cloths of different colours and materials. They were adapted according to use from cloaks to togas, and certainly looked vibrant, though I have doubts what actual benefit they offered to the drama in question. Nevertheless, building up a store of materials like this may prove beneficial in the future.

NON-SPECIFIC ITEMS

These are props without any specific or obvious use in the drama. The sponge pipe insulation used for water pipes is an excellent example of this. It can be an atomic bar, an ancient amulet, or an animal tranquilliser.

Non-specific items are excellent substitutes for items integral to a drama, when the genuine article is not available, or doesn't even exist! They offer a physical bridge when an imagined item might not be successfully employed. These props can be found by purposeful looking, but are largely found by accident in garages, lofts or boot sales. Among the best items I have found were an old concierge bell from a hotel, and a two-colour bottle filled with bath oils. The latter has been a poison, a medical remedy, a life-reviver and used as a token of peace in its time, and was bought in a health shop for 90p!

SPECIFIC ITEMS

Similar to the above, specific props are those which are essential to the drama, and are easily available. If a computer disc is called for in a drama, use one!

Again, the potential to go overboard with specific props can prove irresistible to some. Bear in mind that if every child has a need for an item, then 30 will have to be collected. Every prop added to the story increases the work for the teacher, and also the potential for disruption. Keeping the number to a minimum maintains the children's enthusiasm without overworking the teacher.

One regular justification for using a specific item is to enhance the realism of the drama - examine this perspective more objectively; the children are in school uniform, more than likely in their school hall, and are being asked to imagine and re-create events and situations, not make them real! To use an item for this reason is unfounded. It must be remembered that if the focus of the drama is to produce powerful writing, then realism must often come much further down the list of priorities.

ARTEFACTS

While using a genuine historical artefact may be tempting, they are very often either precious or valuable - and usually both! Any use of an item like this must be treated with care and sensitivity; it may even be appropriate for the teacher leading the session to be the only one to have access.

The only real benefit to using an artefact is if it is in-situ. Houses and vehicles are perfect for this, and Museums that are school-friendly are often exceptionally accommodating to those schools who want to enrich the visit further. Among special recommendation is the Weald & Downland Open Air Museum in Sussex, which has a collection of over 20 houses from various periods of British history. It is best to contact the museum in question beforehand, and speaking to their Education Officer for assistance; sometimes the groundwork has already been done for the teacher.

MUSIC

Using music as a prop may be seen as unusual, but can have vast benefits in terms of creating an atmosphere, developing tension or building a scene.

One way to use music is to play the excerpt and discuss what images the children come up with in their head. They can then be linked directly or indirectly to the drama in question. While Smetna's music that recreates the journey of a river is clear to the listener, more vague tunes can also be used to create an impression or effect.

One good source for instrumental music has been found with film scores. Highly accessible, they have been written to create an atmosphere that may well suit the drama perfectly. In addition, they may not be as familiar as conventional classical music for older children. Another good source is rather surprising - theme park soundtracks. More and more major attractions now sell the park music; The Eden Project, the Millennium Dome and France's Futuroscope being just three. They are often entirely instrumental, and have a range of musical styles and tempos on them. Contact the theme park by post or on the Internet for further details.

WEAPONS

No teacher worth his or her salt would risk introducing weapons of any sort into a drama, whether toy or as representation. It is simply asking for trouble!

CHAPTER SIXTEEN

Ways to Record

Although the activities detailed in this book are primarily for use as a spur for creative writing, this can be achieved in a multitude of ways and forms, outlined below.

EXTRACTS

One of the main difficulties in creative writing is the actual structure of a story itself. By asking the children to write an extract, the problematic areas of plot and structure can be forgotten. These often occur naturally with this sort of writing anyway, and can be pointed out to the children in retrospect.

The extract itself can take many forms; it could be the extract from a story, tale or novel; it could be the central or concluding chapter in a book; they could even be a part of a diary (and the more secret, the better).

DIARY WRITING

This is especially effective for a series of drama sessions, where the action takes place over a number of weeks. With so much occurring each time, events and feelings can easily be forgotten, and a diary not only aids this memory, but also is a regular writing task that is useful in practising an informal style.

It is suggested that a separate book is kept for the diary, for the sake of continuity. After each session, outline what events have occurred, and get the children to record these in brief. After this, allow the children some time to make their entry. This could also be used as a "time-filler" for the end of a reading or English lesson.

Through experience, it is wise to read but not mark diaries in the way you might normally mark English work. If a child is pulled up on their grammar or spelling, then the focus is immediately taken away from the creativity, which defeats the whole purpose.

At the end of the series of drama sessions, get the children to read their diary and highlight their favourite sections, and why.

Using the diary method of recording events also lends itself well to book making. Several sheets of A4 paper, soaked in a tea/coffee mix, and stitched together in the middle, adds even more effect to the diary and in turn, the ownership of the writing.

NARRATION

Drama sessions offer a great deal of opportunity for the children to become narrators of the story. Not only do they not get tied to one character but they also have an insider's view of events.

This greatly benefits any normal writing where the story is dictated to the children, or one that they have to create on their own (which is increasingly expected, and exceptionally hard for an adult to do, let alone a child). They have the freedom to choose the mood, direction and events of a story, adjusting what they have been in/seen in any way they choose. It is, in a sense, freedom within boundaries.

PLAYSCRIPTING

This is quite a challenging form of writing, but can have many uses, especially when practising dialogue. Again, the writer has the freedom to either take elements of a conversation they have had, or create entirely new conversations.

The finished scripts are not usually suitable for performance, since they are a result of drama, rather than a prop for drama. In any case, the use of scriptwriting is beneficial for revealing to the teacher exactly what was important to the child in the drama. More importantly, they reveal what was NOT important.

SETTING AND CHARACTER ANALYSIS

After a drama session, the children are bursting with images, feelings and events that are well-suited to more extended work on settings and characters.

It is one thing to write a description of a set character, but it is another to have trod in those footsteps. The writing of characters will not necessarily be of the physical attributes, as might normally be expected of a child's character description. They will more than likely focus on the actual feelings or thoughts of their character, perhaps even their character's opinion on something. Some support may be required for this activity, and one good way to begin this sort of writing is to have a "brainstorm" for a couple of minutes, just to get all the important key words and descriptions down.

Brainstorming also helps when writing a description of a setting. Although there are many good activities for inspiring descriptive settings, nothing beats having been there, and lived through it. Rather like a radio play requires you to add the detail, so the drama session does too.

To create a complete setting for a story involves a great deal of careful thought and order – what works and what doesn't. By experiencing the setting first hand in a drama session, some of the difficult work involved in creating a setting is already done. Like writing a character description, the children will notice many things that they might not normally have done so, in terms of visual appeal, temperature and ambience, and those all-important details which are often thought about afterwards.

RADIO PLAYS

These are often neglected in primary schools today, and yet are very simple to create, write and edit. The facilities needed for creating radio plays exist in almost every school, and the opportunity for children to work in groups without teacher intervention is great. One key advantage is the unusual lasting record that a taped drama can be – and they are of course simple to copy and distribute.

The most effective way of creating a radio play is to firstly record the children talking about their experiences into a microphone. Playing this back encourages the children to listen to their own voice and take on other people's experiences in more detail. There is no reading involved (which is superb in the eyes of those reluctant readers in the class), and yet the children invariably become highly critical of their material.

Subsequent recordings have the benefit of children being more used to using the equipment, and will hopefully use less repetitive language. They might need guidance to create a more structured recording, and perhaps even a narrator, but this merely draws their attention to their content. Presentation and spelling don't even get a look-in here.

Finished recordings can be used to form transcripts, or may even prove to be inspirations for future writing in many genres.

'STILL' RECORDING

This is an exceptional way of recording a drama that should really be seen as a means to an end. Taking a photograph of different key scenes or events can help support any writing work done later in the classroom. A conventional camera works well (especially the excitement of first opening the developed picture envelope), but a digital camera is much more appropriate, since they offer greater flexibility, costing, and the results are virtually immediate to use.

The camera use can be as a continuous record of events, or different elements of the story could be recreated for posterity. The best approach is to create a tableau, that is, a held "action shot" that contains all the elements that either you or the children view as crucial for that scene.

Organise the groups as you see fit, and get them to recreate the event as accurately as they can. The use of asking the children to "freeze" will help this greatly. It must be remembered that this isn't a fashion shoot or an actor's audition; some children may get excited over the camera's presence. A simple "close eyes, relax and become your character" can often eliminate those children who beam adoringly into the camera's lens.

The pictures form an important record for the children, and can support the writing, since they may jog a child's recollection of an event, or indicate that there were many things going on that they didn't notice at the time. Display the photographs prominently, or contain them in a scrapbook or anthology, alongside some of the writing that occurred after the drama session.

FILM SHORTS

These take much longer, and last a couple of sessions in themselves. This is an awful lot of work for the teacher to prepare and organise, so it is not advised for the fainthearted.

Making a film of the drama is ideally suited for those dramas that have stretched over at least a couple of sessions. Discuss with the children all the events, and work out together which are essential to the story or theme. These can then be either recreated and recorded, or some time spent re-enacting them and giving them polish. It is worth warning teachers that the children soon get tired of constantly repeating a scene, and that this is very teacher-intensive. It would be worth having an ongoing task happening at the same time as the filming, to occupy those that are left out at that time.

Once you start involving costumes, locations and props, you are practically staging a play, so only the barest of these is needed. The more costumes and props you add, the more inadequate the children may feel in their roles. It is far better to run the drama as it is, rather than complicate it for the children, or make your own job harder.

One alternative to this is to use a Super-8 camera. Despite their popularity even 20 years ago, they are almost redundant these days, yet are incredibly atmospheric. The cameras are not particularly difficult to borrow, and the film for them can be purchased from a high-street camera shop or developers. The films record only a very short length of time, and cannot be rewound and recorded over. They also don't record sound, leaving you with a silent film. The advantage of the short film is that you and the children only record the most important aspects of the drama, and have to get it right in the first take. I would highly recommend using Super-8, if only to expose this unusual type of film to the children.

WORD PROCESSING & DESKTOP PUBLISHING

With much greater provision being made for ICT equipment in schools, there is a huge opportunity to use computers as ways of creative writing. There are numerous word-processing packages available to children these days, and even the most simple offer children the opportunity to write on their own or as a group. They have greater freedom to edit or develop their writing, and all of it without the use of ink erasers or rubbers!

Similarly, using desktop publishing packages give the children the chance to alter the slant of the story into a newspaper headline or report, a video cover, a magazine article, or even a page for the school yearbook/newsletter. This use of computers not only helps their writing, but also gives them opportunities to enhance or show off their IT skills.

THE INTERNET

With the incredible advance of internet use and technology, it would be a pity not to harness this for creative writing. All the latest Microsoft applications have a facility for saving documents in HTML format, which enables them to be viewed on any internet browser.

There are numerous ways to use this. The children could have a section on the school website devoted to the drama sessions (perhaps including digital still pictures), or even keep their diary using this format.

One interesting use of webpages with creative writing is the creation of a "choose your own adventure" story, where the user chooses between two or more options, and dictates the story. This type of story needs to be well-planned on paper beforehand, otherwise things can get complicated very quickly!

It is not this book's remit to describe the process of creating a series of webpages – there are many other books available that do this far more adequately, and in more detail, than I could. Some of these are listed in the "Further Reading" chapter at the back of the book. Befriending the IT-friendly teacher or technician is often more than enough; they are often all too eager to help out!

SEN PROVISION

There is a much sharper focus these days on children with Special Educational Needs, and this form of inspiration for writing often helps a child with SEN to overcome difficulties they may normally have.

There are many strategies that can be used to aid creative writing, and a few are outlined below;

Shared writing

Now a major feature of the Literacy lesson in schools, this is a collaborative effort by a small group of children, and occasionally scribed by the teacher or a Teaching Assistant. This is a highly effective form of writing, since the children have all carried out the same events, but come together with many experiences and perspectives.

Scribing

One-to-one scribing for a child, especially when using a computer, helps the child that struggles with the act of writing to get their thoughts and feelings down in a way that is instantaneous. One strategy with this is to start the child off with their writing, and leave them to continue or finish it off on their own steam. This takes away the often-horrifying element of the blank page, ready to be filled.

Cartoon Strips

Always a favourite for all ages, and greatly beneficial to younger children or those with SEN, the children record the events using the form of a comic strip (several templates of which are available at the back of this book). The most common method is to draw selected events or scenes, and write an accompanying sentence underneath. This not only creates a record of events, but can also be used in follow up work after the writing. The pictures are able to record what actually occurred, and may encourage writing by using directed questioning; what is that character doing, how do you think the pirate felt, what happened before, or after this picture?

CHAPTER SEVENTEEN

A Host of Ideas

One of the best elements of drama is the scope and variety of ideas you can create, to suit your aim. The diverse range of themes and topics that films, TV and books cover all demonstrate the almost-limitless possibilities available to use for a drama session. More advice on creating a new drama session, like those demonstrated earlier in the book, can be found in Chapter Fourteen. There are six key elements needed for any given situation, and each is described with examples here.

THE TIME

Obviously, your aim for the creative output will in some way dictate the time of the drama, but some allowances can be made. Since it is drama rather than reality, you are free to choose any moment in time, from the genesis of Earth, to beyond present day. Whatever time you occupy, it is valuable to bear in mind any impact this may have on your final creative outcome. Any time outside the children's memory (for example, the Tudors or Wartime Britain) will almost certainly require some preliminary input of some sort. The children need to understand that there wasn't much demand for car mechanics in Viking times!

Try and be as specific as you can about the actual time the events start taking place, as this will have a direct effect on their input and writing. What season do you begin in? What time is it? Some active description in the drama may help this, since some activities the children carry out will be different in summer and winter, or at either end of the day.

THE PLACE

Again, as creator you have carte blanche as to the place. It is preferable to leave some gaps in the information you give to the children, in order for them to fill in. If there is a bedroom, let their imagination decorate it. If there is a pit, let them fill it. Any location that is intrinsic to the outcome does however need more input from those running the activity.

Most dramas thrive on a bed of "community". Whether this community is a group of journalists, or a band of homeless Neanderthals, create a sense of community through the buildings and place. Is it a farmstead, or a giant city? Are the children living on a space shuttle, or in a sleepy hamlet in England?

LOCATION

It is always exciting for the children not to be in their own country, and this should be encouraged. A town in Alaska is very different to one in Saudi Arabia, and the characters will need some time for adjustment to any surroundings that are alien. By focussing in on one difference during a session, other differences may seem less unusual.

It can be helpful to investigate the location prior to the drama itself, with videos and photographs being especially good at this. Although having a location concurrent to a Humanities topic may help in this, be careful not to adjust or skew facts unless absolutely necessary.

The children's ability to compromise on a location never fails to surprise - don't dismiss a place that you may view as being aesthetically unsuitable, this may be far from the truth in the children's eyes. If a vivid enough picture of the imagined location is built up, any inadequacies will seem less important.

Always make sure of the health and safety aspects of any physical location you choose. Whilst it might be exciting to carry out some drama in a nearby woods, ensure that the children are as safe, if not safer, than when in class. Has provision been made for poor weather? Is the leader contactable in emergencies? Sometimes ambitious plans have to be reigned in because of safety concerns. If this is the case, photographs or illustrations of the desired location could be explored with the class, or there could be some recreation of the scene. Some carefully hung blackout curtains (theatrical curtains that many secondary schools may own) and torches in a classroom can make a functional room become a time-tunnel, a cave, or even a blitzed house. If you are unsure of how to create a theme or mood, ask the children; their resourcefulness can be very impressive if they are to benefit.

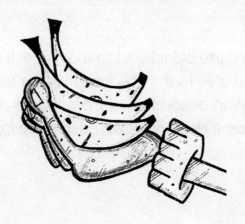

CHILDREN'S ROLES

It is essential that you give considerable thought to the roles that are available to the children in the drama; too few and there will be inevitable frustrations over choice, too many and you could find yourself over-run with unnecessary jobs. Whilst the location is important in making this decision, go through all the possible jobs that would normally be associated with that location. Are there any that are dangerous or inappropriate? Are there jobs that won't have much bearing on the direction you want to take the drama, or conversely, will have the ability to take over the direction of the journey?

Although it is important that the children have a role, it is quite feasible to have active and passive roles. As the 'Rings of Destiny' drama earlier in the book demonstrates, children with passive roles can have an excellent, unusual perspective of the drama as it is carried out. The Guardians (passive roles) in that session are used as sages, dispensing advice to those still surviving the tasks. This use of passive role is best suited to those children who have specific difficulties with group environments, or are painfully self-aware. Being passive in the initial drama may well encourage these children to desire a more active role in the next session.

One cliché that the children will regularly fall into will be to assume the role of "child." This is to be expected, since their range of influence is in many ways more limited than when they are older, but this should be supervised carefully. If taking this role leaves them to simply be a child, playing on the floor, then what benefit will this give to their creative writing? Ensure that in whatever drama you are presenting, even the smallest children have a genuine role to play in the drama; this can be helping the adults, keeping lookout, or even guarding something secret. If necessary, make the other roles appear far more appealing than playing a child - after all, they get to play this role all the time, and will get bored of it very quickly.

OTHER ROLES

There are two quite distinct roles that the teacher can play in a drama session. Whilst there are other roles that can be created or adjusted to suit, they are likely to fall into one of these two categories:

Narrator

More popular, since it requires the teacher to show little, if any, acting prowess, the narrator guides the drama along, explaining or describing each situation to the children, and ensuring that the ensuing events are heading towards the expected conclusion. This is a role much like a class teacher would be used to, but demands a ready answer for any questions thrown at them during the session. Thorough knowledge of the session details therefore is essential.

Teacher-in-role ▨▨▨▨▨▨▨▨▨▨▨▨▨▨▨▨▨▨▨▨▨▨▨▨▨▨▨▨▨▨▨▨▨▨▨▨

This is when the teacher, or another adult, is acting in one of the roles from the drama. This could be as a leader, a priest, a slave-runner, a member of royalty, or even as "one of them" albeit with more knowledge and height! It cannot be stressed enough that in no circumstances should you ever become the person highest up - always be number two in the ranking. If you don't, then you will have nothing to bargain with during exchanges with the children. This offers an excellent way of rebounding suggestions for alternative directions to the drama by the children - "I'm sorry, but the King wouldn't allow us to risk that type of escape" - without offending them, or feeling that all their thoughts and feelings are rejected by the teacher in charge.

It is possible to swap quite easily between these two roles, several times if need be. In one session, it could be possible to be the narrator of the story, and several key roles in order for the drama to progress efficiently. Some teachers may not be in any way driven toward the latter role, the children certainly appear to appreciate it more, and it shows that it isn't just "kiddy stuff" that they're doing.

THE OPENING SCENE

This is crucial in defining the tone and pace of your drama session, and should awaken the children's imaginations, and inspire them to keep with a story or situation that may at first be strange or confusing to them. Think carefully about the scene as a representation of the session as a whole. Any good opening scene in a book, play or film begins with some form of action, and a lot of questions that need answering. Your drama should be no exception to this, to think about what activity the children will begin doing, and also their motivation for doing it. If the story is explained to the children beforehand, there is no surprise to discover along the way for them, and their enthusiasm will soon drain.

Keeping this in mind, ensure that all subsequent scenes don't then appear to be dull by comparison. Think about the momentum that an opening scene or event gives, and then maintain this momentum (or even increase it) in future scenes. Make sure that each scene has a specific purpose and direction, even if this isn't clear to the children at first.

JOINING ALL THE ELEMENTS UP

There are many other aspects to a drama that you can consider and develop, but the six key aspects detailed are the ones most essential to providing a purposeful, enjoyable session for both the teacher and the children. If at any point when looking at the six elements you become unenthusiastic or struggle with the planning, then file the ideas for future consideration and begin again. Very often a chance conversation or TV clip will inspire new and more exciting ideas to develop further, and you should consider each idea to be evolving rather than locked and stagnant.

Many of the drama sessions in this book bear little relation to their original format. 'The Paper Aeroplane' for example, started life as some drama work using a book of the same name as inspiration. Gradually, the book seemed to be more of a hindrance than an aid, and it was quietly withdrawn. Books can still be good sources of ideas and scenes for drama sessions, as long as a sense of perspective is kept about them. Simply because you are using an extract for inspiration, doesn't mean you have to feel a sense of loyalty to an author's ideas; challenge them as much as possible - perhaps you can do much better.

One way to monitor this is to keep a small book of ideas, for use in the future. You would have a place to write down any thoughts, phrases, locations or situations that could be used in a drama session. This could also be a useful book to keep with the children in your class if you chose to.

Other places you can get ideas for drama sessions include:

- television programmes and films
- plays on the radio or stage
- magazines, newspapers and advertisements
- works of art, museums, tourist attractions
- conversations, discussions and internet chats
- shops, markets, shopping centres
- books, diaries, notes, graffiti, correspondence
- holidays, visits, relatives and visitors

SECTION THREE

Additional Information

CHAPTER EIGHTEEN

Material and Templates

The following pages are examples, forms and templates referred to in previous chapters.

ELVIS PARSLEY

This is a sample storyline for the newspaper writing exercise. It is aimed at younger children, and creates a funny story.

BOSLEY BYPASS

This is similar to above, but is more issue driven, and so is more suitable for older primary children.

GROUPING CHILDREN

This template helps the teacher to split and group the children in a session.

FOLLOW-UP FORM

This form helps to establish the success or otherwise of a drama session, and feeds directly from Chapter Thirteen

SESSION DESIGN FORM

This aids a teacher who is designing his or her own session.

Elvis Parsley

Copy the statements below for each group,
then cut each separately, and place in each group's envelope.

Chipshop owners face ruin after shop is destroyed

Elvis Parsley in intensive care

'Too many chips', says doctor

Potato farms double their stocks

Firemen still searching through the wreck

No food found on the scene

Elvis's clothes found ripped in back of shop

'He was even drinking the fat', said onlooker

Police investigate fraud and battery at shop

World tour cancelled - caterers are upset

Bosley Bypass

Copy the statements below for each group,
then cut each separately, and place in each group's envelope.

'It will run over sacred ground', says vicar

200 new jobs with building work

Architect sacked after plans found faulty

Children's playground to close

Tourist boost due to bypass plans

Environmental groups complain to MP

Major supermarket shows interest in bypass

House prices fall around bypass area

Traffic plans to reduce fatal accidents

'When will it end?' ask the elderly

Grouping Children

Team A

-
-
-
-

-
-
-
-

Team B

-
-
-
-
-

-
-
-
-

Team C

-
-
-
-

-
-
-
-

Follow-up Sessions

Spend five minutes briefly answering these questions as honestly as possible, in order to evaluate the progress of the children, and the success of the teaching.

- ❏ **What was unresolved at the last session?**

- ❏ **What would you like to occur in this session?**

- ❏ **Are there any areas to explore?**

- ❏ **Are there any areas to avoid?**

- ❏ **How do you want this session to end?**

- ❏ **How will you go about achieving this?**

- ❏ **What will be unresolved at the end of this session?**

- ❏ **How will this session support the children's creative writing?**

- ❏ **What ways do you want the children to record the events of this session?**

Session Design

❑ **What type of writing do you want to produce?**

❑ **Decide on the eventual outcome of the drama session.**

❑ **How will this be achieved?**

❑ **What situations would help?**

❑ **How will you run the session?**

❑ **Does this cater for the entire group?**

CHAPTER NINETEEN

Further Reading

Although none of these are referred to in the book, and their perspective may be slightly different, they all have some very interesting ideas and philosophies on using drama as an educational tool.

Bolton G.	**Drama as Education** Longman Group, 1984	
Bolton G.	**Towards a Theory of Drama** Longman Group, 1979	
Bolton G.	**New Perspectives on Classroom Drama** Simon & Schuster Education, 1993	
Bolton G.	**Selected Writings on Drama in Education** Longman Group, 1986	
Byron K. (Ed),	**Drama in The English Classroom** Methuen & Co. 1986	
Cook H.	**The Play Way** Heinemann, 1917	
Courtney R.	**The Dramatic Curriculum** Heinemann, 1980	
Davis D. & Byron K.	**Drama Under Fire - The Way Forward** in 2D Autumn, No. 8. (1988)	
Day C. & Norman J. (Ed),	**Issues in Educational Drama** Falmer Press 1983	
DES	**The Teaching And Learning Of Drama** HMI, 1990	

DES	**Drama (Education Survey 2)** HMSO, 1967.
Dunlop F.	**Human Nature, Learning and Ideology in British Journal of Education Studies** Vol. XXV, No. 3. October pp. 239 257, (1977)
Fleming M.	**Starting Drama Teaching** David Fulton Publishers, 1994.
Gillham G.	**Condercum School Report** Newcastle-upon-Tyne LEA, 1974
Heathcote D. (Contributor)	**Chlidren and Drama** David MacKay, 1975
HMSO	**Drama from 5 to 16** 1989
Klein, Melanie	**The Psychoanalysis of Children** London: Hogarth, 1932
McGregor L. (Ed.)	**Learning Through Drama** Heinemann, 1977
McGregor L.	**Developments In Drama Teaching** Open Books Publishing. 1976
Nixon J. (Ed.)	**Drama and the Whole Curriculum** Hutchinson, 1982
O'Neill C.	**Drama Guidelines** Heinemann, 1976
Siks G.	**Drama With Children** Harper & Row, 1977
Wilson A. & Cockcroft R.	**Some Uses of Role-Play as an Approach to the Study of Fiction** Wakefield LEA (n.d.)